Evanston
A Tour Through the City's History

Evanston
A Tour Through the City's History

Margery Blair Perkins

Compiled by Barbara J. Buchbinder-Green
Edited by Barbara J. Buchbinder-Green and Jenny Thompson

ISBN 978-0-615-77179-3

Originally published in 1984 by Chicago Review Press as *Evanstoniana: An Informal History of Evanston and Its Architecture.*

Evanston sesquecentennial edition

All photographs not otherwise credited are reproduced from the collections of the Evanston History Center

Cover Photograph: 222 Church Street, Home of H. H. C. Miller, Evanston, IL, 1887. Collection of the Evanston History Center

Contents

Introduction to the New Edition

Evanstoniana is a book that has been cherished for nearly three decades. People who were born and raised in the city, people who now live in other places, and newcomers to the city have found Margery Blair Perkins' story of Evanston to be both informative and charming.

For many years, Evanston History Center staff have received requests from people who wanted to purchase a copy of *Evanstoniana*, which was first published in 1984. The stockpile of copies quickly dwindled and yet the requests continued to come in.

In honor of Evanston's 2013 sesquicentennial, the Evanston History Center decided to issue a new edition of the book. With the exception of some slight alterations, done primarily to update information, and in some cases to update terminology, the original text is preserved as it appeared in the initial publication. A welcome addition to this new edition includes an index by address of the properties mentioned in the text. A handful of photographs from the original edition are not included in this edition, while some photographs differ from those in the original edition. In some cases, the original image could not be located, and in others, copyright restrictions led us to look for substitutes.

In 2012, many of the properties that appeared in *Evanstoniana* were photographed for this new edition; only two structures whose photographs were included in the original edition were no longer extant by the time this edition was assembled. The former Georgian Hotel on Davis Street and Hinman Avenue, which had been converted to senior housing by Mather LifeWays, had been torn down; a new structure now stands in its place; and, the house at 1560 Oak Avenue, designed by Evanston architect Stephen A. Jennings, was severely damaged by a fire in March of 2011 and eventually razed.

Many people and organizations contributed to this publication. Thank you to the Evanston Community Foundation for its support of this project. Many thanks to Evanston Photographic Studio for graciously allowing use of several photographs, and to Northwestern University for providing scanning services for the project. I am grateful to Melinda Logan, who quickly and flawlessly typed the entire manuscript. Thank you to Matthew T. Marchione for the tremendous amount of time and skill he brought to many facets of the editorial process, including his work on the index and on copyediting the manuscript. Sandra Gross donated her time and expertise to the copyediting process and we are all grateful for her work. A special thank you is due to Vanessa Miceli, who worked tirelessly on researching the photographs in this book. I greatly appreciate all of the hours, effort, and talent she put into this project. For their contributions to this project, I also wish to thank the wonderful staff at the Evanston History Center: Eden Juron Pearlman, Executive Director; Karen Alvarez, Museum Specialist; Steve Brunger, Building Manager; Jan C. Halperin, Director of Development; Erin Hughes, Curator; Janet C. Messmer, Costume Curator; and Lori Osborne, Archivist. I am greatly indebted to Kris Hartzell, Director of Visitor Services and Facilities, who provided the list of Daniel Burnham's work in Evanston (which has been added to the original appendix) and also brought her vast knowledge of architectural history to the editing of this new edition. With the assistance of Hayley Helms and Hannah Van Loon, Kris also compiled the new architectural index for this edition. The book's original editor, Barbara J. Buchbinder-Green, so ably assembled the book's materials, and her work is still noted and appreciated. Many thanks to my husband, Don Souhrada, for helping me with so many and varied aspects of this project. Finally, I would like to thank the members of the Perkins family, especially Julia Perkins Califano, for their support of this project. Margery Blair Perkins and the whole Perkins family have been such an integral part of Evanston's history and their love for the city brought forth wonderful work. We are all lucky that they called Evanston home.

Jenny Thompson, PhD, Director of Education, Evanston History Center, 2013

Foreword to the New Edition

Margery Blair came to Evanston and architecture by marriage. She grew up in Buffalo, NY, studied history and government at Cornell University and law for a year at the University of Hamburg, Germany, and then married Evanston native Lawrence B. Perkins in 1932 and eventually moved to the house at 2319 Lincoln Street that her father-in-law Dwight H. Perkins built for his family in 1904.

Dwight Perkins was a leading prairie school architect as well as an original sponsor and planner of the Chicago Forest Preserve system. He designed numerous public buildings and schools in Chicago as well as many homes in Evanston and the Oakton Elementary School, the original Lincolnwood School and Evanston High School. Larry Perkins was a founding partner of the Perkins and Will Partnership, an architectural firm first known for its schools, including the Dawes School and additions to Evanston High School. When the Baby Boom ended and there was less need for new schools, the firm turned its focus to hospitals and office buildings, including the First National Bank in Chicago.

Midge and Larry raised four children in the house on Lincoln Street and took in numerous relatives, exchange students, refugees and friends that Midge shepherded through the high school and nearby colleges.

Midge was active in the League of Women Voters, managed several mayoral and aldermanic campaigns, taught Sunday school at the First Congregational Church, was a Cub Scout and Girl Scout leader, an active gardener, enthusiastic traveler and photographer and a dedicated volunteer and board member at the Evanston Historical Society, now the Evanston History Center.

She always believed that Evanston's great strength was its diversity: a university town with a strong business community, an active citizenry, a beautiful lakefront and parks and an incredible variety of residential neighborhoods, and with her interests in both history and architecture, she began to document the houses around her, their architects and original owners. She often shared her research and photographs with various civic organizations in Evanston, and the photographs and notes for those lectures became the core for *Evanstoniana*, which Barbara J. Buchbinder-Green completed after Midge died in 1981.

In her lifetime, Midge wrote thousands of letters, kept journals and gave slide and movie lectures on her various interests and travels by car, train, plane and the sailboat she and Larry sailed on Lake Michigan, Lake Huron and Lake Superior as well as the sailboats of friends on which they crossed the Atlantic three times, sailed the North Sea and Japan's Inland Sea and circumnavigated the Mediterranean. She wrote the way she spoke, and in reading her notes and letters, it is easy to reimagine her, sitting in the living room on Lincoln Street, sharing a cup of tea and her interests with a friend, family member or neighbor. She loved her adopted city, was invariably optimistic and would be thrilled today to see the pride of place so many Evanstonians still take in their community and its beautiful homes and gardens.

Julia Perkins Califano, March 2012

Foreword to the Original Edition

Margery Blair Perkins
July 19, 1907--September 7, 1981

For nearly thirty years Margery Blair Perkins was one of the Evanston Historical Society's principal assets. Midge, as she was known to all, was a welcome presence, for whatever she undertook was accomplished with a cheerful enthusiasm that was contagious. She was, in the words of an admiring co-worker, "a major motivator of the whole volunteer program." She first came to the society in 1952 seeking help for a Girl Scout project. Two years later she was elected to the board of trustees and served in various capacities over the next twenty-three years. A grateful society elected her trustee emeritus in 1977.

During her long tenure Midge was tireless: she would propose a project, organize it, work on it, and recruit others to continue it. In 1958 she suggested organizing a women's auxiliary, an idea that took form two years later with the founding of the Guild of the Evanston Historical Society at a tea for 400 guests. She envisioned this group as a working organization of women who would give their time and talent to build a strong society. The unqualified success of the guild has proven her vision correct.

As chairman of the House Committee, Midge guided the society in its move from 1735 Railroad Avenue to the twenty-eight-room lakefront mansion that had belonged to former Vice President Charles Gates Dawes. The vast collection that had been growing since the society's founding in 1898 had to be moved and readied for a public opening. The move took place in June 1960, and after monumental effort on the part of the committee and the board of trustees, the house opened in October. During those first years in Dawes House, Midge initiated or participated in the establishment of procedures and record-keeping systems that remain integral to the society today: the biographical file, the architectural index, and the photograph collection. Midge served as chairman of the Membership Committee, overseeing the greatest period of growth in the society's history.

It is not an overstatement to say that a generous measure of credit for what the society has accomplished during the last twenty-five years is due to Midge Perkins. Only its continued growth and success can repay her and all the others who have given so generously of themselves, for its very existence has always depended upon the talent and dedication of a few extraordinary people. There is no doubt that Midge was one such person.

Mikell C. Darling, Former Executive Director of the Evanston Historical Society, 1984

Editor's Preface to the Original Edition

This book is an affectionate tribute to Margery Blair Perkins and the contributions she made to the city that she loved. Over the years she wrote letters, conducted interviews, took photographs, and read myriad books and documents in order to glean information about Evanston's social and architectural past. As she incorporated what she learned in the files of the Evanston Historical Society, she also kept in mind a larger purpose, that of utilizing these facts in what she called her "house book." However, at the time of her death she had completed only a first draft.

I first came to know Midge, as she was familiarly known, in 1977 when I began attending meetings of the Evanston Preservation Commission, of which she was a founding member. With my interest in Evanston's history and my training as an art historian, I joined the commission's efforts to survey and evaluate Evanston's vast store of architecture and had the opportunity to collaborate with Midge on a number of studies that the commission initiated. When Marvin D. Juliar, president of the board of trustees of the Evanston Historical Society, asked me if I would accept the responsibility of editing her manuscript to prepare it for publication, I felt that I would have the opportunity not only of thanking Midge personally for all she had done, but also of making a contribution to the society.

In the course of editing Midge's manuscript, I had to organize her voluminous notes and compile information from newspaper accounts, biographies, obituaries, real estate listings, building permits, general histories, and the like in order to trace her thought process and provide some of the source material lacking in earlier books on Evanston. As her husband Lawrence B. Perkins hoped, "Her light touch has not been lost," and both he and I believe that Midge's many friends will feel that they are recalling one of her famous slide talks. The book is highlighted by photographs from the archives of the Evanston Historical Society, many previously unpublished, as well as by photographs that I took especially for this book[1], copies of which I have donated to the society's collection. I have also prepared captions to augment Midge's text.

Working with the Perkins family to produce a finished book that would be true to Midge's draft and contribute to the knowledge of the history of Evanston was both rewarding and enjoyable. The wit, geniality, and humor of Larry Perkins made him the most delightful of taskmasters. His suggestions and those of his gracious daughter, Blair Perkins Grumman, have been incorporated along the way, while the other Perkins' children—Dwight H. Perkins, L. Bradford Perkins, and Julia Perkins Califano—also had the opportunity to review the manuscript before it was submitted to the publisher.

I would like to express my appreciation to the board of trustees of the Evanston Historical Society for its support and generosity, especially Marvin D. Juliar, president from 1980 to 1984, and Joseph H. Blake, who took over the reins in June 1984. Those who made donations to the society in Midge's name made it possible to have the edited manuscript typed and to start the process of bringing it to publication. I would like to thank Mikell C. Darling, executive director, who made the facilities of the society available to me day and night to bring this project to its conclusion. I also greatly appreciated the help of Margaret Nicholsen and Mildred Batchelder in proofreading the galleys. Finally, I would like to thank my husband, Raymond J. Green, first vice president of the society, for his forbearance during the many months that I worked both nights and weekends in addition to long days.

On this, the third anniversary of Midge's death, may this book serve as a memorial to the gentle but persistent woman who touched so many others.

Barbara J. Buchbinder-Green, 7 September 1984

Chapter 1

From Grosse Pointe to Ridgeville

Evanston had its beginnings as a rural community of farmers, hungry for land. Some people came west from New England and other eastern states because the land their ancestors owned could not support additional families; others were newly-arrived immigrants from famine-hit Ireland and strife-torn Germany, rent by the political crises of mid-century Europe. Before any of these newcomers could hold title to the land, however, the United States government had to negotiate treaties with the Native Americans, especially the Potawatomi, who had occupied the swampy ground for generations.

The first non-Native American settler, Stephen J. Scott, though he did not remain here long, soon discovered this ownership problem. En route from Buffalo in 1826 on the schooner *Sheldon* with his family, Scott had an argument with the ship's captain, perhaps over passage money or a card game. At the promontory named Grosse Pointe by French explorers many years before, the angry captain put Scott and his family unceremoniously ashore in the wilderness with their baggage. Scott evidently decided that fate had set him here and proceeded to build a temporary "post and pole" cabin, hung with long blankets and pieces of bark, even though he did not have a valid claim to the land. The log cabin that Scott and his two sons built later was the family's home for five successive winters. In 1829 his only daughter Parmelia married fur trader John Kinzie Clark and they set up housekeeping in a log cabin nearby.[2]

That same year the federal government negotiated the Treaty of Prairie du Chien with the Chippewa, Ottawa, and Potawatomi. Scott's cabin was in the southeast corner of the 640 acres awarded to Archange Ouilmette, the half-Potawatomi wife of the French Canadian fur trader and "jack of all trades," Antoine Ouilmette, one of the first white men to arrive on the site of Chicago. To protect the Ouilmettes from unscrupulous land speculators, the treaty forbade Archange and her heirs from selling any of the land without first obtaining the consent of the President of the United States.[3]

The low bluff overlooking the lake stretching north of Scott's cabin all the way to the ridge had long been the site of a Potawatomi village and cemetery.[4] The Native Americans and the rugged French voyageurs who paddled the fur traders past Grosse Pointe on the way to the trading post at Fort Dearborn at the mouth of the Chicago River favored the west side of Lake Michigan because of its southward-flowing current. The arduous but profitable fur trade had been the most important economic activity throughout the nation since early colonial days.

In December 1674 Father Jacques Marquette, in poor health and ailing, camped here on his return journey to establish a mission among his beloved Illinois Native Americans. He wrote in his journal, "December 3, having said holy mass and embarked, we were compelled to make a point and land on account of floating masses of ice. And the next day we reached the mouth of the Chicago River."[5] In Marquette's opinion the area held little promise for the future: "The land bordering on the lake is of no value, except on the prairies."[6] After Marquette's death in May 1675 another Jesuit priest, intrepid Father Claude Allouez, traveled past Grosse Pointe in spring 1677 on his way to take Marquette's place. In November 1679 the renowned French explorer René-Robert Cavelier, Sieur de La Salle, also paddled along the Lake Michigan shore, accompanied by Father Louis Hennepin, two other missionaries, a Native American hunter, and fourteen Frenchmen, on the way to the mouth of the St. Joseph River, where they hoped to build a fort and establish another center for the fur trade. They had four large canoes filled with trading goods, pots, tools, and guns. The following year Henri de Tonti, La Salle's faithful lieutenant, wounded and dismayed by the loss of La Salle's ship, *Le Griffon,* on Lake Erie, struggled on foot through the winter cold, north toward Green Bay, existing on the wild onions he had to dig out of the frozen ground.[7]

Andrew Jackson had been elected president in 1828 on a platform that promised removal of all the eastern Native Americans to western lands. In the spring of 1830 Jackson's "Indian Removal" program became the law of the land. Two years later the Sauk chief Black Hawk led a rebellion of the Sauk, Fox, and Kickapoo, who fought in vain to reoccupy part of their land on the Rock River in defiance of Jackson's order. The federal troops who fought this war with Black Hawk brought news of the fertile lands in which they had skirmished back to their hometowns. By 1833 the Potawatomi began to realize that an influx of white settlers was inevitable; in return for cash payments and grants of land they signed the second Treaty of Chicago and agreed to give up the remainder of their land in Illinois. They moved to the high places of the west, into the forests of Wisconsin, and to the shores of Lake Huron in Canada, thereby finally clearing the way for settlers to obtain valid land titles.[8]

On August 4, 1830, surveyor James Thompson filed a plat of the 267-acre area that would become Chicago. It was to be the northern terminus of the canal connecting Lake Michigan with the Illinois River at Ottawa. The state of Illinois planned to finance the building of the canal by selling square-mile sections of the land on either side of the canal route. The Erie Canal already connected the Great Lakes with the Hudson River, the Atlantic Ocean, and the whole eastern seaboard. The Illinois and Michigan Canal would complete the vital link to the Mississippi River system and the Gulf of Mexico. Land speculation was rampant. When it was incorporated as a town on August 12, 1833, Chicago had a population of about 350. By the time it was incorporated as a city in 1837, the land within Thompson's plat had increased in value a thousandfold to $2,650,000.[9]

Among those who thronged to the frontier town in 1833 was Major Edward H. Mulford. His son James H. Mulford had the first store in Chicago that offered jewelry, art goods, and pianos for sale. In 1835 Major Mulford paid William Bloom $60 for a claim north of the Native American boundary line along the Green Bay Road between what would become Oakton and Howard streets in latter-day Evanston. To protect his claim he built a rough board cabin near the present site of St. Francis Hospital. The first year he rented it to the pioneering Arunah Hill family. Hill, with his wife and seven children, sailed from Cleveland to Chicago on the schooner *Dolphin*; they arrived in Grosse Pointe in a wagon pulled by an ox team. The ten-mile trip from Chicago had taken twenty long hours. Mulford and his wife Rebecca moved to Grosse Pointe in 1837 after Hill built his own cabin further north along Green Bay Road. About 1841 Mulford was able to purchase the 160-acre claim from the government for $1.25 per acre.[10]

Green Bay Road was perhaps the most important north-south thoroughfare between Fort Dearborn in Chicago and the trading post at Fort Howard near Green Bay, Wisconsin. The trail had been worn down through the woods to the depth of about a foot over the centuries. In 1832 Congress authorized construction of a post road along the old Native American trail. Improvements were slow, however, and stagecoach service did not begin until 1836. Lathrop Johnson, proprietor of the first coach service, used an open lumber wagon drawn by four horses. The journey between Chicago and Milwaukee took a day and a half. During the summer there was tri-weekly service; in winter, daily. By 1845 Frink, Walker & Company operated four-horse post coaches and stage sleighs every day. They dominated the stage and mail service of northern Illinois for a decade and a half, although there was competition. During the summer, however, people preferred to travel by boat rather than suffer the jarring bumps and wet stream fordings along the rugged trail.[11]

Rebecca Johnson Mulford (1794-1873) and Major Edward H. Mulford (1794-1878) were the first permanent settlers in Grosse Pointe. In 1858 they would become two of the six founders of the Evanston Baptist Church. Their portraits, painted before they left New York, still belong to the Mulford family.

The Mulford's home, "Oakton," built ca. 1845 at 250 Ridge Avenue, was the social center of the Grosse Pointe-Ridgeville period. Mulford was known as the "gentleman pioneer" because of the large library he had amassed in his home. The house was demolished in 1963.

Across from his cabin Mulford built a 30 by 40 foot log house where he opened a tavern—the Ten-Mile House—as a stopover for the coaches and people traveling along Green Bay Road. As the first justice of the peace in Cook County, Mulford held court in his tavern or often in the open air.[12] In 1846 the Mulford home was also used for the first post office for the Grosse Pointe district with George M. Huntoon, another new arrival, as the first postmaster.[13]

During the next decade other pioneers, immigrants from England, Ireland, and Germany, as well as from Luxembourg, traveled in covered wagons, by sailing ship, and even on foot from Buffalo and Detroit in search of a better life for their families—among them, the Murphys, the Reeds, the Carneys, the McDaniels, the Crains, the Didiers, the Pratts, the O'Learys, and the Huntoons. In 1839 Paul and Caroline Adams Pratt took up 140 acres on the ridge; a year later Caroline Pratt gave birth to a daughter, Susan Pratt [Leonhardt], the first child born to any of the pioneers. Charles and Osro Crain settled on the ridge near latter-day Greenleaf Street. George Washington Huntoon bought land on the ridge between the Crain brothers and Edward Mulford. Huntoon built the first frame house in Grosse Pointe. Other settlers, the Burroughs, the Fosters, and the Jellersons bought land further north along the ridge near present-day Noyes Street. In 1848 Isaac Burroughs, a carpenter by trade, built the Buckeye Hotel on the north ridge; it became another stagecoach stop and community gathering place. When the post office was moved there in 1848, David Burroughs, Isaac's brother, was appointed postmaster; he brought the mail on horseback from Chicago once a week.[14]

Newcomers were always welcome because a "house raising" meant a community celebration. William F. "Uncle Billy" Foster, who came from Ireland by way of New York, was usually the life of these house raisings. His continuous stream of stories and jokes entertained the workers from dawn to dusk. Billy Foster built his own house on the north ridge near what would later become Grant Street.[15]

Paul Pratt (1807-1896) came to Grosse Pointe from Boston in 1839 and bought 140 acres of land, bounded by present-day Church Street, Asbury Avenue, Simpson Street, and Maple Avenue. The son of one of the Minutemen of the American Revolution, Pratt sold logs and lumber from the trees he felled.

Caroline Adams Pratt (1816-1895) descended from the Adams family that gave the United States two presidents. On September 18, 1840, she gave birth to the first child in the fledgling settlement.

Lucinda Boler Huntoon (1796-1875) and George Washington Huntoon (1792-1884) arrived in Grosse Pointe in 1839 and had a cabin built at what would become the northeast corner of Ridge Avenue and Main Street. Courtesy George William Huntoon.

Many of the first houses were made of logs, with mud filling the chinks. Those skilled in handling an axe split logs into shingles for roofing and into boards for doors and shutters. To help keep out the cold, window openings were covered with paper made transparent by greasing the surface; glass later became available for windows. There were plenty of boulders with which to build a fireplace; mud and clay filled the gaps between the stones. Across the top of the chimney the pioneers suspended hams, bacon, and beef for smoking. Later cabins were made of logs hand hewn on two or four sides, carefully notched at the corners to fit. Some people even improved their cabins with sawed boards and paint.[16]

The settlers sold the wood they cut as they cleared the land. Wood filled the holds of small schooners on their way to Chicago. Ox teams hauling wood jostled along the roads, bad as they were. The oak and ash that the settlers cut also made good stock for kegs, pails, and well buckets. There were a number of cooperage shops along the ridge: that of Charles and Osro Crain was near what would later become Greenleaf Street.[17] When the railroad came through in the 1850s, its engines also needed wood; long rows of cordwood soon lined the right-of-way near the stations. After most of the wood was cut, farming, and growing vegetables to sell in Chicago succeeded as the principal activity on the land the settlers cleared.

During the early days foxes, deer, and raccoons wandered in abundance and wild passenger pigeons filled the woods. The settlers captured the pigeons in nets and sold what they did not need themselves for food or feathers. They considered Eli Gaffield the best "pigeon fisher" in the area. He built his first house on the ridge south of the Crains.[18] Gaffield and the Crains were among the thirty men from Grosse Pointe who went west in the 1850s to seek their fortunes in the California gold fields. Some were quite successful and bought more land when they returned.[19] Gaffield, who bought twenty-eight acres on the north ridge as early as 1844, had a new house built, probably after he returned from California. Moved in 1923 to 1232 Simpson Street, Gaffield's house survives as a relatively unchanged example of the Greek Revival style.[20]

Charles Crain, who came to Grosse Pointe in 1843, married Sarah Burroughs, the sister of Isaac Burroughs, in 1846. Returning from the California gold rush with a fortune of $1,600, he purchased various parcels of real estate. After selling one tract in 1872 to Julius White for $10,000, the Crains built the large Italianate house that still stands at 1046 Ridge Avenue. Photograph by Charles Aikin.

Osro Amandor Crain (1819-1898), the elder brother of Charles, purchased twenty acres on the ridge in January 1844 for $5 an acre. In 1845 Isaac Burroughs built a six-room house for Crain and his wife Olivia, the daughter of Arunab Hill. It cost $300 and "surpassed in size and pretension any other residence on the Ridge Road north of Chicago" when it was finished. In 1874 it was moved to 815 University Place.

After Eli Gaffield returned from the California gold rush he had an elegant Greek Revival house built at 2123 Ridge Avenue. In 1923 it was moved to 1232 Simpson Street.

The Greek Revival style had started in England in the early nineteenth century, inspired by the discovery of the Elgin marbles and the renewed interest in Greece, then fighting for independence from the Turks. *The Antiquities of Athens*, a collection of measured drawings of Athenian temples by two Englishmen, James Stuart and Nicholas Revett, published in 1825, furthered the interest. When Grosse

Pointe settlers had enough money they sought to build Greek Revival houses like those they left behind in New England, New York, Pennsylvania, and Ohio. There were no architects among them, but there were carpenters who were able to copy classical details from house pattern books, modifying the designs when necessary to meet their skills as well as the client's purse. Two of the most popular books were *The Practice of Architecture* by Boston architect Asher Benjamin and *The Beauties of Architecture* by New York architect Minard LaFevre.[21] These carpenters who moved west could not reproduce columned Greek temples on the Illinois prairie:

> *So the average house was boiled down to one with narrow pilasters on the corners instead of the portico, a low gable instead of a pediment, and a cornice instead of an entablature . . . Further economy was effected by omitting even the cornice across the end walls under the gables, returning it only a matter of a foot or so. This small piece of cornice on each side of the front and back of a building is the surest indication of the Greek Revival style before it completely disappeared about 1855 or 1860 . . . An equally eloquent symptom is the profile of the mouldings . . . In those days there were no factories for the making of moulded trim, doors, stairs, etc. . . . These Greek shapes are very characteristic and are instantly recognizable when you get to know them. On the old pioneer bonuses they occur in the cornices around the door and window openings and on the interior trim.[22]*

These houses had flat or low-pitched roofs like Greek temples and seldom had a porch unless the house was a mansion.[23] Early settlers did not bother to put up elaborate columned porticoes, which were more common in the East and in older Illinois towns like Galena and Belvidere. It was a simplified form of the Greek Revival, to be sure, easy to build, unostentatious, and favored by farmer and professor alike. These houses, three windows wide, with an uncovered stoop, required only a small lot and often turned a gabled façade to the street. On occasion, however, some, like the Buckeye Hotel, had their long side toward the street. They were usually painted white or cream and had green shutters and trim.

More innovative than the style or architecture was the method of construction, invented in Chicago as many other construction techniques would be. Half-timbered houses of late medieval times and early houses in the America colonies were framed with heavy posts braced with diagonal timbers, with all the lumber adzed and sawn by hand. Long horizontal timbers had to be slotted or mortised to accept floor beams, and all framing had to be spiked or pegged together: "all this, doubtless, made a strong house, but it was a tedious, expensive and wasteful method of construction...."[24] About 1833 George Washington Snow thought of a simpler way, which was called the balloon frame.[25] Sawmills, driven by steam instead of by water or ox-driven wheels, could turn out smaller pieces of lumber:

> *In this form of construction the carpenter took these slender 2 x 4 and 2 x 6 studs, set them on end the entire height of the wall, and placed them about sixteen inches apart on centers and jointed their tops together with another 2 x 4 laid horizontally. Instead of "mortissing," that is, fitting the heavy floor-beams into hugh girts, he laid the ends of these joists, two inches in thickness, on a slender "ribbon"—a 1 x 6 board let into the sides of the studs. Holes for windows and doors were cut out wherever desired, and 2 x 4 rafters were set about 20 [inches] on center, their ends resting on the plate. After the "frame" was completed, the builder had a light wooden cage which he proceeded to enclose with a covering of boards called "sheathing."[26]*

It was light construction, but very strong. Invention of the cheap, mass-produced nail had made it possible, because builders formerly had to use hand wrought nails. There was also a plentiful supply of lumber from the great white pine forests of Michigan and Wisconsin. In the opinion of architect John Wellborn Root:

This early type of dwelling has made the growth of the West possible . . . Unlike the early dwellings of wood erected in the East no expert carpenter was needed—not mortise nor tenon nor other mysteries of carpentry interfered with the swiftness of its growth. A keg of nails, some two by four inch studs, a few cedar posts for foundations, and a lot of clapboards, with two strong arms to wield the hammer and saw—these only were needed, and these were always to be had.[27]

The farmers who came from Germany and Luxembourg and tilled the black soil west of the ridge developed another method of building. Because the low land was so wet, they used brick for the ground story, where they sheltered their tools and even some of the farm animals. An outside wooden stairway led directly from ground level to the second floor, which was built of wood and usually covered with clapboards; the second floor was the family's living quarters. Many of these early farmhouses survive, frequently altered and enlarged, but the one at 1400 Wesley Avenue retains much of its original character.

The Luxembourg farmhouse, a vernacular building type that could withstand flooding in low-lying areas, is found throughout Evanston. Although the majority have been drastically altered, the one at 1400 Wesley Avenue has retained much of its integrity. Photograph by Jenny Thompson.

By 1850 there were enough settlers to organize a township, which they named Ridgeville at the town meeting held in April of that year. The little post office adopted the same name. Meanwhile, as they set up their new town and cleared and tilled their land, a coterie of nine Chicago men began to look for land for quite another purpose. In the mid-nineteenth century churches throughout the nation were taking the leadership in founding colleges. These Chicagoans, successful in their respective professions and businesses, were all still in their thirties and all were Methodists who desired to establish an institution of "sanctified learning" in the states carved out of the Northwest Territory. This group included Dr. John Evans, a professor of obstetrics whom the eloquent preacher, the Reverend Matthew Simpson, had converted to Methodism several years before; Orrington Lunt, a successful grain commission merchant; and lawyer Grant Goodrich.

John Evans, born in Ohio of Quaker parentage, was a man of many interests. Before Evans moved to Chicago in 1848 he lived in Indiana where he successfully lobbied to establish the first institution for the mentally ill, rescuing these unfortunates from confinement in jails. He was asked to join the faculty at Rush Medical College in Chicago. He was on the editorial staff of *The Illinois and Indiana Medical and Surgical Journal*; in 1849, after studying the path of the virulent cholera epidemics plaguing Chicago, he wrote an article declaring that cholera was contagious and that a quarantine law should be passed. He would become one of Chicago's leaders. Always interested in education, he promised to reform the public school system in Chicago when he was elected alderman in 1852. He became a friend of Abraham Lincoln and heartily supported opposition to slavery and helped found the Republican Party in Illinois, which promoted Lincoln's presidency in 1860 on an antislavery platform.[28]

John Evans (1814-1897), who gave his name to Evanston, graduated in 1838 from Cincinnati College. One of the founders of Northwestern University, he had an interesting and varied career. When President Lincoln appointed him governor of the Colorado Territory in 1862, he moved to Denver.

Orrington Lunt, who emigrated from Maine to Chicago in 1842, began his business career as a commission merchant. Purchasing his first set of account books on credit, he bought and sold anything he could—from cranberries to grain. Chicago quickly became the grain center of the continent: "in 1856 nearly nine million bushels of wheat and twelve million bushels of corn passed through the city's elevators."[29] Lunt, a charter member of the Chicago Board of Trade, made enough of a fortune that he was able to retire young in order to manage his real estate interests. Lunt "exercised a potent influence in the city of his adoption. Every enterprise calculated to further its prosperity deeply interested him." He was a director or trustee of many of the institutions organized to make Chicago a better place. In 1897, on the day of his funeral, Chicago closed its schools; in Evanston, flags flew at half mast.[30]

In addition to a successful career as a commission merchant Orrington Lunt (1815-1897) was a charter member of the Board of Trade, lobbied Congress for improvements to the Chicago harbor, and took an active role in many civic and business institutions. He devoted his life to philanthropic and political work, not the least of which was Northwestern University.

Grant Goodrich was a lawyer, judge of the Superior Court, and an ardent temperance man. Like Evans he was interested in the public schools and a friend and supporter of Abraham Lincoln. He was also active in one of Chicago's volunteer fire groups. In 1837 he helped organize the Mechanics' Institute "to diffuse knowledge and information throughout the mechanical classes."[31] "Keen, combative, persistent" Goodrich served as chairman and chief advisor of the founding group.[32] The other six were Jabez K. Botsford, the owner of a hardware store; the lawyers Andrew J. Brown and Henry W. Clark; and representatives of Chicago's three Methodist churches—the Reverend Richard Haney of the Clark Street Church, the Reverend Richard K. Blanchard of the Canal Street Church, and the Reverend Zadoc Hall of the Indiana Street Church.[33]

Grant Goodrich (1812-1889) came west from New York in 1834. Elected first president of the board of trustees of Garrett Biblical Institute, he served in this capacity for thirty-five years. He and his wife Juliet Atwater Goodrich moved to Evanston ca. 1855-56 and lived on the west side of Hinman Avenue between Clark and Church streets, but moved back to Chicago a year or so later.

On May 31, 1850, at a meeting in Goodrich's law office, situated over Botsford's hardware store, these nine men took the initial steps to found a university of "sanctified learning" under the aegis of the Methodist Church. The nearest college at the time was Knox College in Galesburg and there were only three other colleges in the state—McKendree at Lebanon, Shurtleff at Alton, and Illinois at Jacksonville. During the next session of the Illinois legislature they secured a charter for Northwestern University that was approved by Governor Augustus C. French on January 28, 1851. Appointed as trustees were founders Grant Goodrich, Orrington Lunt, John Evans, Jabez K. Botsford, and Andrew J. Brown, as well as Alson S. Sherman, mayor of Chicago in 1844 and one of the founders of the Mechanics' Institute; George F. Foster, chandler and sailmaker, Chicago alderman, president of a volunteer fire company, and vice president of the Anti-Slavery Society; John M. Arnold; Absalom Funk; E.B. Kingsley; and Eri Reynolds, who died shortly thereafter and was replaced by Dr. Nathan Smith Davis.[34]

That June the board of trustees met to organize; they decided to begin with the establishment of a preparatory school. At subsequent meetings they urged the Methodists in the Northwest not to establish additional colleges, but to concentrate their energies on building Northwestern into a great university.[35] On June 23, 1853, they selected the Reverend Clark Titus Hinman, who was not quite thirty-four years old, former principal of the Methodist Conference Seminary in Newbury, Vermont, and later principal of Wesleyan Seminary in Albion, Michigan, as the first president. Hinman was a popular preacher, "a man of wonderful energy; nothing ever waited with which he had to do."[36]

The Reverend Clark Titus Hinman (1819-1854) was chosen in 1853 to be the first president of Northwestern University. During his brief tenure he planned courses, started an endowment drive, and began the search for members of the faculty.

The trustees needed a site for their campus. They gave up the idea of the city site that they had already purchased, thinking it perhaps more desirable to establish their school away from the city's many temptations. Hinman, who was not interested in just an academy or high school for Chicago, but in a university for the whole Northwest, suggested the committee look along the roads and railway lines. For a time land in Jefferson (a suburb developing west of the city) tempted them. Orrington Lunt, who had always dreamed of a site on Lake Michigan, persuaded the others to hold off their decision on the Jefferson site until they had visited Ridgeville. On July 4, 1853, they tramped through the marshy land until reaching a grove of large oaks, which Lunt had discovered on an earlier trip beside the silver-blue lake. He said they threw their hats in the air and shouted, "This is the place." The wilderness lay all around them, and the land they desired belonged to Dr. John H. Foster, a Chicagoan who was not at all interested in selling.[37] Evans and Lunt, however, proved persuasive when they actually met the exorbitant price of $25,000 for his 379-acre farm. Evans agreed to pay $1,000 of his own money and put his name on a ten-year mortgage at six percent interest for the rest.[38]

From the beginning the university founders wanted to guide the development of the village that they were confident would grow around their school. They anticipated no trouble in attracting newcomers, for during the 1850s people in Chicago were already looking for greener pastures, fresher air, and less crowded and healthier neighborhoods in which to live. Chicago was dusty and hot in the summer, damp the rest of the year, crowded, and unhealthy. Hordes of rats lived under the wooden sidewalks of the sprawling frontier town filled with rootless, rough, careless men and women who drifted through life, waiting for something better to turn up. Only a few streets were paved and fire was a constant danger.[39] It was a time of development all over the Chicago area. Even as Northwestern was being founded, Paul Cornell, a young lawyer whose wife was the sister of the wives of John Evans and Orrington Lunt, was buying 300 acres south of Chicago to establish the suburb he would call Hyde Park. Cornell's sister was married to George Kimbark, who became an officer and director of the company that would plan and develop the town of Riverside.[40]

At one time a circuit preacher and later pastor of the Clark Street Methodist Church in Chicago,
the Reverend Philo Judson (1807-1876) was appointed business agent of Northwestern University on October 1, 1852. In
April 1854 he bought Alexander McDaniel's house at the northwest corner of the ridge where Church Street would later
cross and moved to Ridgeville.

The Northwestern trustees appointed the Reverend Philo Judson business agent and asked him to plat a new village. In addition to the Foster farm, Judson included in the plat the adjoining 28-acre Samuel Billings farm, which the trustees purchased for $3,000, and the James Carney farm, 248 acres on the ridge that trustee Andrew J. Brown purchased for $13,000 in his own name. Judson himself bought the property of pioneer Alexander McDaniel at the northwest corner of the ridge where Davis Street would later cross, but excluded it from the plat. Judson surveyed the land over the winter of 1853-54, setting aside areas for parks and the university campus and arranging the streets in a grid pattern roughly parallel and perpendicular to the lake shore and the two ridges, which were named Ridge and Chicago avenues. Where Sherman and Orrington avenues met at Davis Street, Judson provided an open space as a breathing area for the village, the beginning of the central business district. Judson also laid out alleys. John Evans wished the village to bear the name of the famed Methodist preacher, the Reverend Matthew Simpson. Others, however, believed that is should bear Evans' name. His wife Margaret Gray Evans gave final form to the name ratified by the university trustees, and "Evanston" was the name submitted on the 1854 plat. The streets were named in honor of the university founders and trustees, prominent Methodists, pioneers and early settlers, and geologic and natural features.[41] Lake Michigan was the eastern boundary, Wesley Avenue was the westernmost street, Crain and Hamilton streets formed the southern border, and Foster Street the northern.[42]

The first Northwestern building, which the trustees asked Chicago's first architect John Mills Van Osdel to design, was erected at the northwest corner of Hinman Avenue and Davis Street.[43] On June 15, 1855, they dedicated the Preparatory School. Graced with a wooden tower and bracketed cornice, the building contained six classrooms, a chapel, a library, a small museum, and halls for two literary societies. However, Clark Hinman did not live to see it go up; he died on October 21, 1854, of typhoid fever, the result of overwork, before the fledgling university could open.[44]

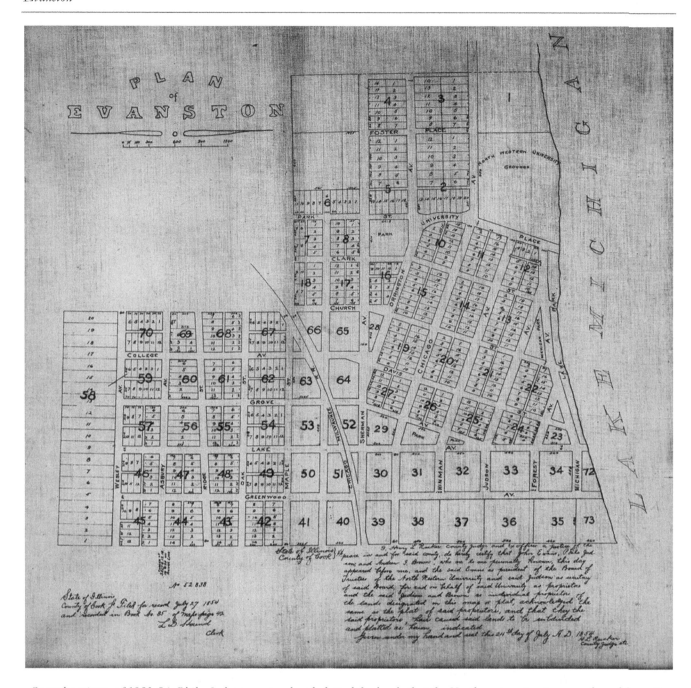

Over the winter of 1853-54, Philo Judson surveyed and platted the lands that the Northwestern trustees purchased from Dr. John H. Foster and Samuel Billings and that Andrew J. Brown bought from James Carney. The plat of Evanston was submitted to Judge Henry L. Rucker on July 24, 1854, and recorded three days later. The Illinois legislature changed the name of Ridgeville to Evanston on February 15, 1857.

Northwestern's first structure, the Preparatory School, was built at the northwestern corner of Hinman Avenue and Davis Street. Dedicated June 15, 1855, it was designed, according to Thomas Eddy Tallmadge, by Chicago's first architect, John Mills Van Osdel (1811-1891). Photograph by Alexander Hesler.

To commemorate the centennial of American Methodism, Garrett Biblical Institute built Heck Hall in 1866-67. After a devastating fire on February 23, 1914, the site was eventually cleared and Deering Library built almost two decades later. Photograph by Alexander Hesler.

While Northwestern's trustees were busy arranging for platting their lands and selling perpetual scholarships to raise money, the Reverend John Dempster, another gifted Methodist preacher, visited Chicago. Dempster had been associated with the first theological seminary for the Methodist Church at Newbury, Vermont, although he complained that he had met "fierce and persistent opposition on the part of at least two-thirds of our entire ministry."[45] In 1853, on his way to assume the presidency of a new Methodist college at Bloomington, Illinois, he stopped in Chicago to speak at a meeting favoring higher education for ministers. Several of Northwestern's trustees were in the audience. As Grant

Goodrich had already persuaded Eliza Clark Garrett, widow of former Chicago mayor Augustus Garrett, to bequeath her money to endow such a Methodist training school, the Northwestern trustees were able to persuade Dempster to establish his seminary close to their new school. The state legislature granted Garrett Biblical Institute a charter on February 15, 1855, and four directors of Northwestern—Grant Goodrich, Orrington Lunt, John Evans, and Philo Judson—and Stephen P. Keyes were named trustees. Goodrich was elected president and served for thirty-five years; Lunt became secretary of the board. Dempster Hall soon rose near the north edge of the university campus, but Eliza Garrett died not long after its dedication in January 1855.[46] In 1866-67 the Garrett trustees built a commodious dormitory, Heck Hall, named for Barbara Heck, the "Mother of Methodism in America." Its $60,000 cost was financed by the money-raising efforts of the American Methodist Ladies' Centenary Association.[47]

The Reverend John Dempster (1794-1863), a Scotsman, accepted the challenge of the presidency of Garrett Biblical Institute after serving as a circuit preacher, as a missionary in South America, and as an educator. In 1862 he urged President Lincoln to emancipate the slaves. When he died he was buried on the grounds of Garrett, but was reinterred in Rosehill Cemetery three years later. Photograph by J. Carbutt.

Daniel Parish Kidder (1815-1891) and his wife Harriet Smith Kidder (1816-1915) came to Evanston in 1856 and built their home at 1717 Chicago Avenue. A graduate of Wesleyan University and a missionary in Brazil from 1837 to 1840, Daniel Kidder became the first professor of theology at Garrett Biblical Institute and its second president.

When Northwestern Female College's first structure burned down, the school held classes temporarily in the Buckeye Hotel until their new five-story building on the west side of Chicago Avenue between Greenwood and Lake streets was ready in the fall of 1857.

A third institution, a college for women, was also in the formative stages, although Northwestern's trustees were none too happy at the prospect.[48] Education for women was a radical idea in the early nineteenth century, because men thought women unable to profit from higher education. Oberlin and Antioch colleges had begun admitting women in 1837 and 1843 respectively.[49] But in 1854 the twenty-three-year-old Reverend William Patterson Jones appeared on the scene, anxious to start a woman's college in the Chicago area. With financial backing from his family he organized the Northwestern Female College. On the same day that the Northwestern University trustees laid the cornerstone for the Preparatory School—June 15, 1855—the same ceremony was being held three blocks away on the west side of Chicago Avenue between Greenwood and Lake streets for Northwestern Female College's building. The Reverend Matthew Simpson spoke at both ceremonies. On Christmas Eve 1856 Northwestern Female College burned down: a fire caused by a faulty furnace not only destroyed the building but also invalidated the insurance policy. The Jones family rallied once again and the school was rebuilt, opening again nine months later.[50]

William Patterson Jones (1831-1886), who was born in Philadelphia, graduated from Allegheny College in 1853. After serving as principal of the Peoria Female Academy, he came to Evanston, determined to start a woman's college; in June 1855 he saw the laying of the cornerstone of Northwestern Female College.

No sooner was the plat recorded than those attracted by the university began building houses, especially on the two ridges where it remained dry enough all year round. A number hailed from eastern Vermont. Hannah Bayley Pearsons, whose husband John built one of the first houses within the platted village, had been a bridesmaid at Clark Hinman's wedding to Martha Morse.[51] Henry Sanborn Noyes, the first professor of mathematics, had been a faculty member at the Methodist Conference Seminary of which Himan had been principal.[52]

In 1855 John Evans moved from Chicago and built a board-and-batten Gothic style house facing the lake north of Clark Street. Here he resided and helped guide the new school until President Lincoln appointed him Territorial Governor of Colorado in 1862. When Evans departed to begin his new task, Orrington Lunt took over as the university's guiding light, although Evans remained chairman of the board of trustees until his death in 1897.[53] Produce commission merchant Allen Vane and his wife Mary, who both hailed from Maryland, moved here in 1855, bringing with them a fifteen-year-old African American girl named Maria Murray, whose freedom they had purchased from Mary Vane's family.[54] They built their home at the northwest corner of Davis Street and Forest Avenue; in 1902 it was moved to 1808 Lyons Street.

Many of the houses of the university and seminary professors clustered on streets nearest the lake—Judson, Hinman, and Chicago avenues—where lots cost only five to ten dollars a front foot. One of the most handsome was the spacious residence of Daniel Parish Kidder and Harriet Kidder at 1717 Chicago Avenue, built in an elaborate classical style with a veranda across the front. Kidder was professor of practical theology at Garrett Biblical Institute. The Kidder home was the first house that a new student was likely to visit, "the social center of old-time Evanston." Men and women of prominence mingled here with the poor and obscure.[55]

John Lourie Beveridge (1824-1910), who was brevetted a brigadier general at the close of the Civil War, served as governor of Illinois from 1873 to 1877. The son-in-law of Philo Judson, Beveridge came to Evanston in 1854 and built a home at 1745 Chicago Avenue. When he returned from Springfield he had a larger house built on the same site; it survived until 1972.

At 1745 Chicago Avenue stood the home of John Lourie Beveridge who arrived in 1854. Married to Philo Judson's daughter Helen, Beveridge would subsequently go to Congress and later become governor of Illinois.[56] Dr. Jacob Watson Ludlam also arrived in 1855 and bought ten acres on the ridge from his friend Major Mulford. Tall and with polished manners, Dr. Ludlam was probably the best educated in the medical profession among the early doctors.[57] Arriving the same year to minister to the sick was Dr. Fayette Montrose Weller, who settled further north.[58] The founder of Northwestern's Medical School, Dr. Nathan S. Davis, settled on Hinman Avenue, opposite the present-day First Methodist Church. He dedicated his life to improving medical education and was one of the founders of the American Medical Association, as well as of the forerunner of Mercy Hospital in Chicago. The principal business street was named for him.[59]

Wealthier families built their mansions on the ridge. Not that they did not appreciate the beauties of the lake, but in a day when tuberculosis was so common, they feared the harmful effects of the lake air. Lawyer Harvey B. Hurd had a substantial frame house built on Ridge Avenue at the southwest corner of Davis Street; it was completed in spring 1855.[60] Popular Dr. James V. Z. Blaney, who was on the Rush Medical College faculty with John Evans, moved out from Chicago when he joined the Northwestern faculty. In 1857 he had a large frame house built at the southwest corner of Ridge Avenue and Lake Street, which was the scene of many elegant receptions.[61]

Philo Judson built a store facing the open space at Orrington Avenue and Davis Street. James B. Colvin soon moved in, becoming the first merchant with his "anything-and-everything shop."[62] Until Colvin opened his emporium there was no store except for the small supply of groceries available at the Buckeye Hotel. The wife of Professor Henry Sanborn Noyes, acting President of Northwestern after Hinman's sudden demise, recalled that during their earliest days:

Even the mail came only twice a week at first, brought out by a man from Chicago on horseback . . . There was no market, but a butcher came twice a week from Chicago. There were no paths, and, in places where streets were laid out, the deep mud bore the placard "No Bottom." There was a deep ditch through the wetland between the east and west ridges, with one crossing. For two years I went up and down the other ridge for family supplies—eggs, butter, milk, etc.[63]

Much of the year the land between the two ridges lay under water. Major Edward H. Mulford and Edward Murphy constructed the first drainage ditch midway between and parallel to the two ridges. People referred to it as "Mulford's ditch," but in later years students called it "the Rubicon," because it emptied into the lake between the Northwestern campus and Dempster Hall, the first building on the Garrett Biblical Institute campus.[64] Drainage of the land was urgently needed. The farmers needed to drain the land if they were to plant and harvest their crops and keep their cows from becoming mired in the thick mud. The university needed it in order to sell lots to raise money to support itself. And the town needed it in order to build roads connecting the two ridges.

In 1855 the first Drainage Commission was formed. Lawyer Harvey B. Hurd became the secretary and oversaw the operation. At that time the only road on the prairie west of town ran north and south along the eastern edge of the Big Woods to Chicago by way of Bowmanville. It was passable only part of the year—late in summer and in winter when the ground was frozen. When the commission dug the first ditch on the west side of this road, the dirt was added to the road. In spite of the obvious need, "the Big Woods people came out with pitch forks and clubs and tried to drive off the engineer and his workers, but the engineer was firm and held to his purpose."[65]

The Drainage Commission then excavated the Big Ditch between the Big Woods and Ridge Avenue. To the north the water emptied into the lake; to the south the water drained into the North

Branch of the Chicago River three-quarters of a mile northwest of Bowmanville. As they dug other ditches in the prairie, they used the excavated dirt to build roads:

> *One of them is the Rogers Road, commencing just west of what was then the home of Philip Rogers, after whom Rogers Park was named, running thence west to Niles Center. Another is the Mulford Road; another extended on Church Street west to the Big Woods, and another was the Emerson Road, now Emerson Street . . . The Commission enlarged the Mulford Ditch so that it furnished pretty fair drainage for the territory lying between the east and west ridges in the Village of Evanston until the sewerage system was put in.*[66]

Subsequent efforts of the Drainage Commission to build a ditch to drain the Skokie swamp were met by citizens protesting assessments for the improvements. In January 1870 the Supreme Court declared the Drainage Commission unconstitutional, but the Illinois Constitution of 1870 remedied the situation by permitting the General Assembly to pass laws regulating drainage.[67]

Throughout the years there were experiments with almost every kind of paving material. The first attempt to improve Green Bay Road was by laying logs, cut when the land was cleared, to provide a foundation in the mud. But most of the early roads were made of clay brought from the ditches dug in the prairie and then topped with gravel. Every time it rained the gravel became further mired in the clay. Davis Street, which connected the two ridges, became a "hogwallow." When macadam pavement on Davis Street was found to be unsatisfactory, brick was laid on top of it. On Chicago Avenue north of Davis Street a double layer of brick laid on sand was quite successful. Street paving would always be a problem; some people opposed it because they feared city improvements. James Ayars once declared that Hinman Avenue would probably never be paved because it suffered from "too much brains on the street."[68]

Public transportation was also essential to the growth of the community. Chicago's suburbs were growing along the railroad lines that stretched like spokes of a wheel from the center of the city. Andrew J. Brown, the university founder and trustee who purchased the James Carney farm, made sure that one of the railroads would pass through town by donating the station site and right-of-way. Thus, by encouraging the Chicago and Milwaukee Railroad to run close to the college campus, he increased the value of his own property at the same time. In December 1854 a single train began operating every morning and evening into Chicago. There were so few passengers at first that the company debated whether to continue these suburban specials. When they offered more frequent trains and better service, the number of passengers soon increased. There were no sidewalks in the new village, no street lamps. Commuters who wanted to find the way home from the station in the evening left lanterns in the station in the morning.[69]

People also carried lanterns to church services, where "the rich and the poor met together," in the log school that the pioneers had built in the early 1840s on the ridge where Greenleaf Street would later cross. At one service in 1854, Hannah Bayley Pearsons, Helen Judson Beveridge, and her mother were "the only women that had on bonnets such as ladies wear now; the rest had on large sunbonnets and were dressed in primitive style." There were only fourteen people in the congregation. The minister, who was en route to Minnesota, was "a tall, lank individual, dressed in dark blue cotton overalls, with large patches of new cloth on each knee, while the rest of the cloth had been washed until it was almost white."[70] Services were held in the chapel in Dempster Hall of the Garrett Biblical Institute from January to May 1855, when they were transferred to a second-floor room over Colvin's store at David Street and Orrington Avenue. That November the services were moved to the chapel in Northwestern's first building, the Preparatory School.[71]

Harvey Bostwick Hurd (1828-1906) came to Chicago in 1846 and was admitted to the bar in 1848. After the Village of Evanston was incorporated on December 29, 1863, Hurd was elected first president of its board of trustees. One of the founders of the Evanston Historical Society, he was also elected its first president.

Northwestern's trustees supported the establishment of some of the churches by granting a new congregation a site to build its sanctuary. In the summer of 1856 the Methodists erected their own church at the northeast corner of Orrington Avenue and Church Street. The plain little white clapboard building with green shutters cost $2,800.[72] Though under Methodist direction, it welcomed people of all denominations to hear some of the finest preachers and orators of the day. Northwestern also donated land to the Baptists, the Presbyterians, the Congregationalists, and the Episcopalians.[73] However, among the pioneers, there were several Roman Catholic families. To attend church services they had to travel west to St. Joseph's Church or south to St. Henry's. Not until 1864 were they able to purchase a lot at the southeast corner of Lake Street and Oak Avenue, the beginning of St. Mary's parish.[74]

In 1854 Hurd purchased some land from Andrew J. Brown that was included in the Plat of Evanston and gave the contract to build his house at 1572 Ridge Avenue to the carpenter Albert Danks. Completed in the spring of 1855, it was one of the first grand houses on the ridge.

Andrew Jesse Brown (1820-1906), the law partner of Harvey B. Hurd from 1850 to 1854, helped shape the destiny of Evanston by donating land for the Chicago & Milwaukee Railroad right-of-way and station in 1854. President of the Union Bank and a Chicago alderman, Brown finally moved to Evanston in 1867 and lived at 1505 Oak Avenue.

Built on the northeast corner of Church Street and Orrington Avenue, the First Methodist Church was dedicated on July 27, 1856, with the Reverend John Dempster preaching at the ceremony. In 1872 the structure was sold to the Norwegian-Danish Methodist Church and moved to the southeast corner of Church Street and Sherman Avenue where it remained in service until 1899.

Colvin's Store, on the northeast corner of Davis Street and Orrington Avenue, was the general store operated by James B. Colvin, who had arrived in Grosse Pointe in October 1836. The second floor once served as the meeting place for the congregation of the First Methodist Church.

On February 14, 1855, four years after the university's incorporation, the state legislature amended Northwestern's charter in ways that would profoundly affect the town. One amendment provided that "no spirituous, vinous, or fermented liquors shall be sold under license, or otherwise, within four miles of the location of said University, except for medicinal, mechanical, or sacramental purposes . . . Provided, that so much of this act as relates to the sale of intoxicating drinks within four miles, may be repealed by the General Assembly whenever they make think proper."[75] For nineteenth-century men and women, demon rum was the root of much social evil, an evil they believed they could remove from their environment by education and political action. Temperance was a leading crusade of the day and nowhere was it waged so thoroughly for decades as here. Not everyone was for temperance, however, and the amendment to the university charter engendered considerable debate. Frances Willard later wrote that "the sentiment of the town is so strong in favor of prohibition that the subject of granting licensees has never yet come up in the local elections."[76] The village trustees would later pass a prohibition ordinance in keeping with the amendment. Over the years there would be frequent attempts to break the limitation, as well as numerous legal suits, but Evanston would remain "dry" for over a hundred years, "the ideal temperance town of the great Northwest."[77]

The second amendment stipulated "that all property of whatever kind or description, belonging to or owned by said corporation, shall be forever free from taxation for any and all purposes."[78] The state, unable to provide financial aid directly because of its meager budget, found this the cheapest way to encourage higher eduction.[79] Helpful as the amendment was to a struggling young institution, it planted the seed of complaint that the university did not carry its share of the cost of public services, a seed that would grow into a deeply-rooted prairie flower.

Chapter 2

Evanston: The "Sanctified" Town

On February 15, 1857, the Illinois legislature officially changed the name of Ridgeville to Evanston.[80] Northwestern's founders, who hoped to establish a university dedicated to "sanctified learning," belonged to a generation that believed it could create or at least strongly influence its social and political environment; they therefore wanted a "sanctified" town. The university catalogue of 1858-59, hoping to attract students, extolled the young town: "We have never seen a community anywhere in which so large a preponderance of opinion was strictly moral and religious . . . Parents may send their sons here with the utmost confidence that they will be placed at a distance from temptation and brought under the most wholesome influences."[81]

A "sanctified" town would support freedom and equality of opportunity, regardless of color or sex. Therefore, abolition of slavery, prohibited in states carved out of the Northwest Territory, was a popular crusade, especially among the Methodists.[82] There have long been unconfirmed rumors that Evanston was a station on the underground railroad; John Evans, "if not actually a 'conductor' . . . was known to have assisted runaway slaves in their attempts to reach Canada."[83]

In 1860 Julius White, harbor master of Chicago, invited his friend Abraham Lincoln to visit his Evanston home when he came to Chicago for the "Sand Bar" case. White's neighbor Harvey B. Hurd accompanied Lincoln on the train to Evanston. After a tour of the town, they proceeded to White's house at the northwest corner of Ridge Avenue and Church Street, where Lincoln addressed the assembled crowd.[84] A few weeks later Lincoln received the Republican nomination for the presidency at the convention held in the Wigwam, a two-story frame structure built in just five weeks' time on land owned by Garrett Biblical Institute.[85]

When the Civil War broke out with the fall of Fort Sumter on April 13, 1861, Northwestern students eager to enlist walked all the way into Chicago when they discovered that the last evening train had already departed. After the Union defeat at Bull Run on July 31, Julius White made an impassioned plea to help save the Union and free the slaves. At a meeting the following evening patriots signed the roll and pledged financial support. White himself, whom Lincoln had recently appointed Collector of Customs of the Port of Chicago, resigned in order to enlist. White headed the Thirty-Seventh Illinois Infantry. John L. Beveridge formed Company F of the Eighth Illinois Cavalry and became Colonel of the Seventeenth Illinois Cavalry. William Gamble, who was in charge of harbor improvements before the war, led the Eighth Illinois Cavalry and played a conspicuous role in the decisive Battle of Gettysburg. These three Evanstonians were all brevetted generals. Twenty-four other Evanstonians served as officers of lesser rank, and another fifty-four volunteered in the calls for fighting men.[86]

Julius A. White (1816-1890), who served in the Wisconsin legislature in 1849, was appointed Collector of Customs at Chicago. After serving as Colonel of the Thirty-seventh Illinois Volunteers during the Civil War, he was brevetted a Major-General in March 1865 and returned home to Evanston. Photograph by Brady, New York.

Soldier's Fairs were held in Chicago in the fall of 1863 and in May 1865 to raise money to care for the sick and wounded soldiers of the Union Army. Jane Currie Hoge, who moved to Evanston after the war, devoted all her energies to managing these fairs and with Mary A. Livermore stood at the head of all the women working for the war.[87] An Evanston woman, Sarah Hyde, initiated a petition in favor of freeing the slaves. It bore the names of more women than had ever been enrolled on paper: "*The Northwestern Christian Advocate* in Chicago reported that a mammoth roll, almost beyond the capacity of a man to carry, was being daily added to the petition. Senator Harlan had been engaged to see that the petition was presented to the president, when lo! the Emancipation Proclamation sounded through the length and breadth of the land."[88] Small wonder that free African-American people who moved north during or after the war came to Evanston to find a home. Andrew Scott, who fought in the war, came to Evanston in 1863. Nathan Branch, who also fought in the war, was mustered out in the fall of 1864; after working two years at the Sherman House in Chicago, he moved to Evanston.[89]

On December 29, 1863, Evanston was incorporated as a town.[90] Although people were immersed in the war effort, they elected thirty-five-year-old Harvey B. Hurd the first president of the board of trustees. After adopting its rules, the board's first official act was to pass an ordinance enforcing the university's ban on liquor.[91] But the assassination of President Lincoln on April 14, 1865, just after the war's end, shocked the village. The Reverend Matthew Simpson preached Lincoln's funeral sermon and young Henry Pearsons served as one of the guard of honor while Lincoln's body lay in state in the rotunda of the Chicago courthouse.[92]

Henry Alonzo Pearsons rose to the rank of captain in the Eighth Illinois Cavalry during the Civil War and served as a member of the honor guard when the body of President Lincoln reached Chicago. In 1874 he had a house built at 1718 Chicago Avenue, just north of his parents' home.

A "sanctified" town would provide equal rights for women. So, education for women, an important asset in obtaining equal rights, became a major goal. It had become obvious that Northwestern Female College had not lived up to William P. Jones' expectations and could not provide education of a high enough standard for women. In 1868 Mary F. Haskin, who had a vision of what education for women in Evanston could be, approached several other women with the idea of starting yet another institution. With Mary Haskin as president of this "Educational Association," they persuaded Professor Jones, in frail health after his six-year sojourn in Macao as American Consul, to merge his Northwestern Female College with their new Evanston College for Ladies.[93] They petitioned the town for land and received one of the chief parks.[94] In 1869 the state granted them a charter and fifteen women were named to the board of trustees.[95]

The board elected Frances E. Willard president of the new college on February 14, 1871.[96] In young Frances Willard, eager to build an interesting career although hampered by an authoritarian father who set limitations on her ambitions, they found a persuasive and dynamic leader. She gathered allies in almost all the faculty wives at Northwestern and Garrett as well as among the church women.[97] One of her first tasks was to manage a Fourth of July benefit to raise money for a building. She opened the publicity campaign with an eloquent speech on "People Out of Whom More Might Have Been Made." Ten thousand people came to the laying of the cornerstone on July 4, 1871, many arriving by excursion boat from Chicago. A baseball game between Northwestern and the Evanston College for Ladies resulted in a score of 57 to 4 in favor of the men. The festivities at the Women's Fourth of July raised $10,000; Dr. John Evans, by then governor of the Colorado Territory, gave $2,500.[98]

The remarkable energy of Frances Elizabeth Willard (1839-1898) extended to the causes of education, labor reform, and woman's suffrage, in addition to temperance. She was a prolific author and lecturer and after her death was the first woman honored with a statue in Statuary Hall of the United States Capitol.

Dr. Erastus O. Haven had accepted the presidency of Northwestern in 1869 on the condition that women would be admitted to the university. Upon Haven's resignation in September 1872, Charles Fowler, to whom Frances Willard had once been engaged, was elected president. Although she had differences of opinion with Fowler, Frances Willard continued as dean of the Women's Department when the Evanston College for Ladies was merged into Northwestern University in 1873. Woman's College, the large mansard-roofed building designed by Gurdon P. Randall, was finally completed in April 1874; it became known as the "Fem Sem" and served both as the women's dormitory and a seminary in which a few courses were offered.[99] Northwestern had finally become a coeducational institution that recognized the rights of women to an equal education. Five women became members of the university's board of trustees: Kate E. Queal, Jennie Fowler Willing, Elizabeth M. Greenleaf, Emily Huntington Miller, and Mary Bannister Willard.[100]

Randall also designed Northwestern's first permanent building, University Hall. Construction was begun in 1867 and the building completed in two years:

> *The style of the edifice is gothic with steep roofs. It is surmounted with towers, turrets, mansards, etc. which add much to its picturesqueness. In the main tower, at an elevation of 120 feet, is a lookout from which may be seen on a clear day the towers and spires of Chicago, twelve miles distant. The building is admirably constructed of brick and stone—the latter being rock-face, which gives it a rich, massive and substantial appearance, comparing notably with any university structure in the land.[101]*

Construction of the Evanston College for Ladies, designed in 1871 by architect Gurdon P. Randall, was slowed in the aftermath of the Chicago fire. By the time the building was completed in April 1874 the college had been absorbed by Northwestern University and the building named Woman's College. The imposing Second Empire structure, which had a tower in the original design, was renamed Willard Hall in 1900; it is now known as the Music Administration Building.

Frances Willard suggested that Daniel Bonbright "was the good genius of the building that elder Evanston was wont to call 'a poem in stone.' "[102] Bonbright, a Pennsylvanian, came to Evanston in 1858 to teach Latin language and literature. A profound scholar, he was the most traveled of the new professors.[103] In 1861 Oliver Marcy joined the Northwestern faculty as professor of natural history. He and his wife Elizabeth Eunice Smith Marcy bought a simple clapboard-covered home at 1703 Chicago Avenue that boasted the first wooden sidewalk in town, at a time when sidewalks were looked upon as a frill.[104]

In 1860 George F. Foster had the first brick house built in Evanston at the southwest corner of Ridge Avenue and Greenwood Street. Foster, who had served as a Chicago alderman and a term in the Illinois legislature, was on Northwestern's first board of trustees. In 1863 he sold his Italianate villa of Milwaukee brick to Charles Comstock, the western agent of and partner in the Onondaga Salt Company.[105] In 1864 the Eclectic Club was founded in his home for "intellectual improvement and social enjoyment." It lasted for fifteen years and its membership was limited only by "the seating capacity of our parlors." There were no "restrictions except territorial" and the prominent families of the ridge met

regularly every Monday evening, at the houses of different members in alphabetical order. The exercises consisted of two readings, one by a lady and one by a gentleman each evening, also in alphabetical order. Each reading was not to exceed half an hour, and the rest of the evening was devoted to music, conversation and refreshments. Sometimes a whole evening was devoted to music, sometimes to a Shakespearean Play, sometimes to storytelling, sometimes to a scientific discussion, sometimes to tableaux, and once, at least, to the trial of a member for "high crimes and misdemeanors."[106]

Built 1867-69, the "elegant and commodious" University Hall was Northwestern's first permanent building. Designed by Gurdon P. Randall, the High Victorian Gothic structure of Joliet limestone housed classrooms, offices, a chapel, a laboratory, and a library, with a museum and dormitory space in the attic story.

Oliver Marcy (1820-1899), professor of natural history at Northwestern for thirty-seven years, also served twice as acting president as well as dean of the College of Liberal Arts for twenty years. Not only was Marcy Avenue in northwest Evanston named in his honor, but also the highest peak in the Adirondacks and a species of oak tree. Photograph by Alexander Hesler.

In 1864 Oliver and Elizabeth Eunice Smith Marcy purchased a lot and house on the northeast corner of Chicago Avenue and Church Street. After moving the house as well as its wooden sidewalk, they had this larger house built ca. 1868-69. It was demolished in 1957.

At the suggestion of Henry Bannister several men organized the Philosophical Society in 1866 "for mutual improvement in science and general knowledge." In addition to regular meetings for the membership, which embraced both those connected with the university and interested townspeople, the society held a course of free public lectures.[107] The Henry Bannister family settled in a pretty house at

1627 Chicago Avenue. Bannister was a Hebrew scholar on the Garrett faculty, chairman of the public school board, and an enthusiastic supporter of higher education for women.[108]

Not only was Evanston a community "in which so large a preponderance of opinions was strictly moral and religious," but Evanstonians were also concerned about saving and protecting souls across the oceans to make them just as moral and religious. During the last half of the nineteenth century, explorers, David Livingstone among them, began to open the continent of Africa. On the other side of the world Commodore Matthew Perry appeared off the coast of Japan in 1854 with a United States Navy fleet and forced that long isolated country to open to foreigners. China and India were also "discovered." Interest was keen in these far-away "heathen" lands with strange customs. In 1870 Evanston women organized the Maternal Association, an interdenominational missionary union. Social life seemed to resolve around this group as the women busily raised funds to send missionaries overseas to undertake good works, to preach the Christian gospel, and to bring literacy and better health to the "heathens." Elizabeth Crandon managed to raise $425,000 to send thirty missionaries throughout the world. Others who helped make the missionary movement a success were Kate E. Queal and Mary H. B. Hitt.[109]

The first missionary sent to Japan by the American Board of Commissioners for Foreign Missions was the Reverend Daniel Crosby Greene of Evanston's First Congregational Church; his appointment "naturally fostered a lively interest in foreign missions. . . . Most interesting was the coming here [in 1872] of Sawayama Umanoshin, afterward known as Paul Sawayama. Studying in the university, he united with this church, and studied theology with Dr. Packard during the last year of his stay here."[110] He returned to Japan in 1876 to found a Christian school and college.[111] Many of the students at Garrett Biblical Institute were training for missionary work so the missionary unions always had a ready supply of speakers to impress upon them the importance of their work. Among the Garrett alumni who went into missionary work, the most famous was Joseph C. Hartzell, who later became the Methodist Bishop of Africa.[112] So dedicated were Evanstonians in their support of missionary work that it was said that Mark DeCoudres, at the age of ninety, shingled his house himself in order to contribute $100 to the African missions.[113]

George Franklin Foster (1812-1877), chandler and sailmaker, served a term in the Illinois legislature and as a Chicago alderman. President of one of Chicago's volunteer fire companies, vice president of the Anti-Slavery Society, and one of the founders of the Mechanics' Institute, he was appointed to the first board of trustees of Northwestern University.

The 1855 amendment to Northwestern's charter prohibiting liquor within four miles and the subsequent village ordinance that enforced it drew "a class of people who were total abstainers and who desired for their children the surrounding of sobriety."[114] However, because the four-mile limit extended well into the settlement of Rogers Park and the townships of New Trier and Niles, there were frequent attempts to strike down the limitation. In April 1862 the Illinois Supreme Court heard the case of John O'Leary vs. Cook County. Harvey B. Hurd, representing Northwestern, related "that the attorney on the other side was so drunk that I had to submit his side of the case to the court as well as my own!"[115] At this first test of the constitutionality of the amendment, Chief Justice John D. Caton ruled that "the object of the charter was to create an institution for the education of young men, and it was competent for the Legislature to embrace within it everything which was designed to facilitate the object. Every provision which was intended to promote the well being of the institution, or its students, was within the proper subject matter of that law."[116]

In 1860, on the site of James Carney's log house, George F. Foster had the first brick house in Evanston built. The home of the Comstocks from 1863 until 1905, the house at 1326 Ridge Avenue was sold to banker W. Irving Osborne (1859-1933). Remodeled by architect Jarvis Hunt, "Eastbank" remained one of the most splendid mansions on the ridge until it was demolished in 1941.

Popular sentiment supported this view. Luther L. Greenleaf, born in the tiny village of Derby in northeastern Vermont, moved to Chicago in 1862 to represent the western interests of the Fairbanks Scale Company. Greenleaf, who "knew the blessedness of living outside the sickening atmosphere of the saloon [and] that moral suasion must go hand in hand with prohibition," moved to Evanston in 1868 and helped form the Temperance Alliance.[117] Under the influence of the 1874 women's "Crusade" against liquor, Evanston women founded the Woman's Temperance Alliance on March 17, 1874, and elected Abby McCagg Brown its first president: "among their objects were the prosecution of violators of the university charter law, the circulation of the pledge, and the visiting of all places within the four-mile limit where liquors were secretly sold or gaming was carried on." The Alliance changed its name to the Woman's Christian Temperance Union (WCTU) on May 1, 1875.[118]

Luther Leland Greenleaf (1822-1886), a partner in the firm that would ultimately become Fairbanks Morse & Company, was also a prominent real estate developer. Well-known for his generosity to many local institutions, he was ruined by the 1871 Chicago fire and moved to Beloit, Wisconsin. Greenleaf streets in Evanston and Chicago were named in his honor. Photograph by Alexander Hesler.

The house built for Luther and Elizabeth Greenleaf, 228 Greenwood Street, was far larger and more elaborate than the cottages he had built on lots scattered throughout the town. After a major remodeling in 1928 by Mayo & Mayo, the house no longer bears any resemblance to the original board-and-batten Gothic structure.

Julia Sprague Comstock (1825-1901) and Charles Comstock (1814-1895) came to Evanston in 1861 and acquired not only George Foster's house but also all of Blocks 44 and 45 of the Village of Evanston where they built several houses for speculation along Greenwood Street and Asbury Avenue. Photograph by Charles Aikin.

Like many other businessmen, Greenleaf became wealthy from investing heavily in real estate, purchasing scattered lots on the ridge and near the lake where he had houses built: "Mr. Greenleaf was a man who ought to be remembered by the people of Evanston. He helped a great many people to homes that otherwise wouldn't have got them."[119] The "Maecenas of early Evanston," Greenleaf opened his well-lined pocketbook for every good cause. In 1869 he gave Northwestern University $7,500 to purchase the nucleus of its library—11,246 volumes plus unbound publications that had once belonged to the Prussian Minister of Education, Dr. Johann Schulze.[120] Both Northwestern and the University of Illinois elected Greenleaf to their boards.

Before he became one of the tragic victims of the Chicago fire, losing almost everything despite his wife's valiant efforts to recover some of the family fortune, Greenleaf built an elaborate Gothic mansion at 228 Greenwood Street for his family.[121] Picturesque, asymmetrical in plan, it had vertical board-and-batten siding and elaborate scroll-sawn ornament on the gables and porches. The other houses that Greenleaf had built for speculation were less elaborate than his own and featured small rooms, curving staircases, bay windows, fireplaces of imitation marble, and parquet floors in myriad patterns. A number of these "Greenleaf cottages" survive, although some are shorn of their board-and-batten siding, while others have lost their elaborate bargeboards.

Henry Bannister (1812-1883) became professor of exegetical theology at Garrett Biblical Institute in 1856. He and his wife Lucy Kimball Bannister settled in a house at 1627 Chicago Avenue. After housing the Woman's Exchange Cafeteria for thirty-three years, it was demolished in 1939. Photograph by Alexander Hesler.

Other contractors and carpenters built similar houses in neighborhoods all over town, copying those they had known in their native states or had seen in popular magazines and books of the day because they had neither the skill nor the time to devise their own designs. The most famous Gothic house in Evanston was built by Josiah Willard, Frances' father.

Devastated when his younger daughter Mary died in 1862 at "Swampscott," the first Willard home at the southwest corner of Judson Avenue and Church Street, he decided to build a new house. A stern male chauvinist, Willard did not deign to consult his wife and daughter about moving and even sold all the family furnishings at a local auction, much to their distress.[122] The new house at 1730 Chicago Avenue was ready by 1865; they called it "Rose Cottage," but Frances Willard later changed the name to "Rest Cottage."[123]

Josiah Willard (1803-1868) moved his family to Evanston from Janesville, Wisconsin, in 1857. "Swampscott," built by George Reynolds on the southwest corner of Church Street and Judson Avenue, was the Willard home until "Rest Cottage" was completed in December 1865. When Asa Daggett Reed, the President of City National Bank, purchased the house and decided to build a new home on the site, "Swampscott" was moved to 1562 Sherman Avenue; it survived until 1910 when it was demolished for the Evanston Theater.

"On some new lots reclaimed from the swamp" on Chicago Avenue Josiah Willard built a nine-room Gothic cottage with vertical board-and-batten siding and decorative bargeboards. An eight-room addition to the north in 1878 expanded the house to accommodate the widow of Frances' brother Oliver, Mary Bannister Willard, and her four children. The Woman's Christian Temperance Union has maintained the house, furnishings, and personal memorabilia of Frances Willard since her death in 1898.

Gothic architecture, popularized by English writers John Ruskin and Charles Eastlake and the English architect Augustus Northmore Welby Pugin, began to supplant the Greek Revival in England in the early nineteenth century. Its dissemination throughout the United States was probably due more to the popularity of the books written by the landscape architect Andrew Jackson Downing.[124] Downing's treatises contained designs and plans for the perfect country villa; they were appropriate for a "sanctified" village since he emphasized the good, the true, and the sincere, and his writings had decided religious overtones:

> *There are three excellent reasons why my countrymen should have good houses. The first is, because a good house (and by this I mean a fitting, tasteful, and significant dwelling) is a powerful means of civilization. . . . The second reason is, because the individual home has a great social value for a people. . . . The third reason is, because there is a moral influence in a country home—when, among an educated, truthful, and refined people, it is an echo of their character—which is more powerful than any mere oral teachings of virtue and morality. That family, whose religion lies away from its threshold, will show but slender results from the best teachings, compared with another where the family hearth is made a central point of the Beautiful and the Good.[125]*

Downing also felt that "domestic architecture . . . should be less severe, than public buildings, less rigidly scientific, and it should exhibit more of the freedom and play of feeling of everyday life."[126] He was an advocate of "picturesque" architecture: "The Picturesque is seen in ideas of beauty manifested with something of rudeness, violence, or difficulty."[127] Historians consider Downing important because "he decisively established the principles of asymmetrical, picturesque design in America and thereby laid the foundations for a whole new sequence of experiments in planning and spatial organizations."[128] In addition, he was prophetic and, for the time, novel in his emphasis on labor-saving efficiency and sanitation, advocating a "bathing room" as well as a toilet in every home and devices such as the dumb waiter, the speaking tube, and the rotary pump.[129] Downing considered houses painted white "entirely unsuitable and in bad taste. . . . The glaring nature of this colour, when seen in contrast with the soft green of foliage, renders it extremely unpleasant to an eye attuned to the harmony of colouring."[130] He also preferred porches over the imposing Greek porticoes fashionable during the first forty years of the nineteenth century.

Lawyer Hugh Alexander White (1830-1894), who came to Chicago in 1856, moved to Evanston after having a spacious Italianate house built at 1407 Ridge Avenue in 1867. After a major remodeling by Otis & Clark in 1911 for William S. Mason (1867-1961), founder of the real estate firm of Smith Morse & Mason, it was acquired by Major Lenox R. Lohr (1891-1968) when he assumed the presidency of the Museum of Science and Industry in 1940. Virtually unchanged since 1911, the house survives although surrounded by a cluster of smaller houses on the once spacious grounds. Photograph from Classic Evanston.

Downing also promoted the Italianate villa and emphasized its high moral tone:

What we mean by a villa, in the United States, is the country house of a person of competence or wealth sufficient to build and maintain it with some taste and elegance. [A] villa is a country house of large accommodation, requiring the care of at least three or more servants. . . . the most refined home of America, the home of its most leisurely and educated class of citizens. . . it is in such houses that we should look for the happiest social and moral development of our people. . . it is there that the social virtues are more honestly practised, that the duties and graces of life have more meaning, that the character has more room to develop its best and finest traits than within the walls of cities.[131]

Italianate mansions feature spacious interiors and high-ceilinged rooms with tall, narrow windows:

The hallway was in the center, with a stairway which usually ran in one straight ramp. . . . Opening off the hall on one side through wide folding doors was the parlour. Behind this was the dining room. On the other side, usually of the same size and relationship, ranged the sitting-room and a large bedroom. Each of these rooms was provided with a marble fireplace carved in a debased rococo style, or else made of slabs incised with Eastlake decoration. Plaster cornices surmounted the wall, and in the center of the ceiling was a huge plaster rosette. . . . The arrangement of the rooms on the second floor was similar, except that a single bathroom, long, narrow, and high, accommodated the household. A rear wing housed the kitchen, back stairs and an anomalous room behind the kitchen, which was part laundry and part woodshed. The crowning glory of the house was the cupola. This room, never visited except by the children in fear and trembling, was plastered and finished as the rooms below.[132]

The kitchen had been brought up from the basement and often included a scullery for rough work. Pantries separated the kitchen from the airy dining room in order to eliminate or reduce kitchen smells. Because General Ulysses S. Grant was president of the United States when many of these villas were constructed, in Evanston people often called them "General Grant houses." Built of brick or wood, they had hipped roofs, ornamented window and door frames, and decorative brackets supporting the overhanging eaves. Many sported cupolas set in the center of the roof or towers called belvederes. Although Evanston was once said to have more Italianate villas then any other Chicago suburb, many have been demolished, and only the house at 701 Forest Avenue still retains its belvedere. One of the largest and most prominent of these houses was the mansion that lawyer Hugh A. White and his wife Catherine had built in 1867 on the half block of land between Ridge and Oak avenues at Greenwood Street.[133]

In 1869 a group of villagers visited Northwestern's trustees to protest the university's exemption from taxes. The trustees replied that they were having troubles enough, even with the subsidy, in trying to build a strong school. Grant Goodrich outlined "what the University had done for the town, was doing, and would continue to do. . . and how the scheme of mutual benefits ought at once and forever to quiet the incipient murmurings on the subject of tax-burdens because of the university exemption."[134] In 1874 some Evanstonians filed the first lawsuit against Northwestern protesting the tax exemption granted the university in the 1855 amendment to its charter. Northwestern won, but the feeling against the university's freedom from property taxes persisted.[135]

By 1870 Evanston's population numbered 3,062, more than triple the 831 people who lived in Evanston in 1860. One of the significant events that profoundly affected the development of Evanston was the great Chicago fire, which broke out on October 8, 1871; for three days:

[t]here was going north on Chicago Avenue what seemed to be an endless funeral procession. Closed carriages, broughams, and victories, drawn by beautiful horses, were filled with the sad, homeless people. In many of the carriages all the available space was used for family heirlooms, gold and silver; strapped on top of the vehicles were much-prized family portraits. Every vacant space on the entire shore was most willingly turned over to these highly respected old Chicagoans, many of whom later selected a North Shore suburb for their future homes. The fire made 100,000 people homeless.[136]

Orvis French and his family took some of the refugees into their three-story double house at the northwest corner of Hinman Avenue and Greenwood Street. A number asked to stay until they could decide whether to remain in Evanston or return to Chicago: so began the Greenwood Inn, an Evanston institution for eighty-one years.[137] Other refugees camped on the grounds of Captain John Dorchester at the southeast corner of Lake Street and Forest Avenue.[138]

Born in Vermont, Orvis French (1822-1897) moved to Milwaukee in 1856 and went into the dry goods business. When he quit Milwaukee for Chicago in 1867 he started a wholesale clothing house. Burned out in the 1871 Chicago fire, he turned his Evanston home into a boarding house, the French House.

A few of the refugees who stayed because they liked the ambiance found that Evanston still allowed the construction of wooden houses. Fireproof construction, required by Chicago after the fire, was considerably more expensive.[139] Some of the refugees had wealthy relatives to help them and others were able to rebuild their own fortunes. Silas Kitchell, whose son-in-law Henry C. Tillinghast lived in Evanston on the ridge, decided to stay and soon had the handsome clapboard-covered house at 1411 Maple Avenue built.[140] The fire also finally brought Orrington Lunt to live in the town in which he had been involved for so long. In 1874 he purchased the villa on Judson Avenue at Clark Street facing the lake, which had been built for Melinda Hamline, the widow of Bishop Leonidas L. Hamline, probably just after she moved to Evanston in 1864.[141] Lunt's daughter Cornelia, who "specifically chose as her role in life what may be called aesthetic philanthropy," began at once to expand the cultural life of Evanston, befriending people in music, literature, and art.[142]

Alfred Lorraine Sewell (1832-1913), editor of the children's magazine The Little Corporal from 1865 to 1871, started the Evanston Index in 1872, the town's only newspaper until 1889 when the Evanston Press was born. Sewell lived at 1318 Chicago Avenue until he retired to Niles, Michigan, in 1894. Photograph by Alexander Hesler.

Alfred L. Sewell began publishing the *Evanston Index* the summer after the fire. Its first issue appeared on Saturday, June 8, 1872, and he asked the Chicagoans who moved to Evanston after the fire to send in their names.[143] Another victim of the fire, Thomas C. Hoag, saw his wholesale and retail grocery business destroyed in the blaze. An Evanston resident since 1857, he bought the brick building at the southeast corner of Chicago Avenue and Davis Street in 1874 and opened a local grocery. As treasurer and business manager of Northwestern, he saw the need of a local bank and soon opened a private bank in the rear of his store. Thomas C. Hoag & Company established itself as an Evanston institution; in 1892 Hoag sold his interest to the newly incorporated State Bank of Evanston.[144]

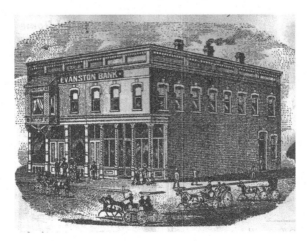

T. C. Hoag & Company, the forerunner of State National Bank, was established in 1874 in the rear of the grocery of Thomas C. Hoag (1825-1906). The building on the southeast corner of Davis Street and Chicago Avenue is still standing and Hoag's safe is part of the collection of the Evanston History Center.

In 1892 Benjamin Bayless purchased the French House, which stood on the northwest corner of Hinman Avenue and Greenwood Street; in 1896 he changed the name to the Greenwood Inn. It was razed in 1952.

"Anchorfast," 1742 Judson Avenue, was built ca. 1864 for Melinda Johnson Hamline (1801-1881), the widow of Bishop Leonidas L. Hamline. The home of Orrington Lunt from 1874 to 1897 and of his daughter Cornelia Gray Lunt until 1934, the house was razed in February 1949.

Cornelia Gray Lunt (1843-1934) was affectionately called "the first lady of Evanston." First president of the University Guild, one of the founders of the Fort Dearborn Chapter of the Daughters of the America Revolution, and a charter member of the Fortnightly Club, she stands in the library of "Anchorfast" next to one of several portraits painted of her.

New subdivisions were laid out and the demand for houses brought many changes: "With the exodus to Evanston, which occurred as a result of the great fire of 1871, a new life dawned upon our heretofore almost idyllically peaceful village. New interests were developed, new methods introduced, new social circles formed and the village began to assume some of the desirable, as well as some of the undesirable, aspects of a city."[145] Although the fire swelled its ranks, Evanston was still rural: because of frequent complaints that cows were annoying people, the village trustee had to take up the question of hiring a pound master to herd the cows.[146]

Evanston began to acquire other services and amenities that made life safer and healthier. Kerosene lamps were the only source of home lighting and feeble street illumination until 1871 when Northwestern Gas Light and Coke Company built a small plant that provided gas for a limited number of homes. When it merged with People's Gas Company of Chicago, gas street lighting came into general use.[147] In 1872 the federal government began building the long desired lighthouse to mark the dangerous shoals off Grosse Pointe.[148] The wreck of the *Lady Elgin* in September 1860 and the loss of all but 98 passengers resulted in organizing a life-saving station at Northwestern; starting in October 1872 with five volunteers, the crew would save more than 400 lives during its existence.[149]

On October 19, 1872, five months after the Illinois legislature passed the City and Village Incorporation Act, Evanstonians re-organized their government. Keeping the village form, they elected a board of trustees at large instead of electing a council of aldermen representing wards. Charles J. Gilbert, a wealthy commission merchant and real estate developer, became the first president under the re-organization.[150] Petitioned by residents of the area, Evanston annexed in 1872 land along the lake north of Foster Street and east of Meridian (Asbury) Avenue up to the New Trier Township boundary. In January 1873 voters approved annexation of contiguous land just west, bounded on the north by Grant

Street, on the south by Church and Foster streets, on the east by Wesley and Asbury avenues, on the west by Dodge Avenue. Within the month the area bounded on the north by Grant and Simpson streets, on the south by Church street, on the east by Dodge Avenue, and on the west by Hartrey and McDaniel avenues also became a part of the village. In September 1874 the village annexed part of the Abraham Snyder farm, a small piece of land on its southern limit bounded by Hamilton and Greenleaf streets, Lake Michigan, and Chicago Avenue.[151]

The 379 acres that the university bought in 1853 for $25,000 had increased in value to at least $3 million by 1873. But in the financial panic of 1873, some Chicago banks temporarily suspended operations and in the aftermath most construction came to a halt. It was a difficult period and prices fell to the lowest level in years. But the *Evanston Index* editor wrote with optimism, "in the long run, Evanston and Evanston real estate will be benefited by this crisis. People will be all the more certainly convinced that the solid earth is the best savings bank and the best bank of deposit. . . . Let us all keep as cool as we can…"[152]

Wealthy people like Charles Gilbert were less affected; he was still able to build one of the most elaborate houses of this period. Its builder looked to France rather than Italy for inspiration: its great mansard roof was inspired by the recent additions to the Louvre by the architects of Napoleon III. Although many houses were once built in this Second Empire style, the Gilbert house at 1812 Asbury Avenue is the last major residential example in Evanston. Completed in 1875, it was said to have been the first in town to have a ballroom and a billiard room; it also boasted the first burglar alarm, installed "on every other step of the front stairs" to frighten the suitors of Mamie Queen, Gilbert's ward, rather than burglars.[153] Under Gilbert's leadership Evanstonians voted in 1874 to build a municipal waterworks. The first Holly pumping engine was named the "C. J. Gibert" in his honor.[154] When the village organized a volunteer fire department in 1874, the first fire engine was also named for Gilbert.

The Second Empire mansion of real estate mogul Charles Judson Gilbert (1829-1900), 1812 Asbury Avenue, was built in 1874-75 at a cost of $25,000. Elected president of the board of trustees when Evanston's government was reorganized in 1872, Gilbert not only platted and subdivided several additions to Evanston but also was the major force in establishing the town's waterworks. Photograph by Jenny Thompson.

The Big Woods, filled with towering oaks, hickories, and elms, covered much of the land to the west and north of Evanston. Because it was swampy much of the year, roads were almost non-existent; where they did exist, they were often impassable. German farmers began settling in the Big Woods at an early date, clearing the land of its great trees for their vegetable gardens. The wet ground dictated the kind of house they had to build. Like their compatriots to the south their farmhouses had a high brick ground story that could withstand seasonal flooding, while the wooden second story was sheathed in clapboards. An outside stair led from ground level to the second floor where the family lived all year round. In drier areas people built simple cottages, sometimes decorated with ornament cut with a scroll saw.[155]

Developers arrived to make their fortunes. In 1867 Chancellor Livingston Jenks, a Chicago lawyer, bought land in this northern area. John Culver, Adlai Ewing, and others followed:

Dr. Kidder owned some land in that region, and used to advertise "Acres cheaper than town lots," but our Mr. Charles E. Browne . . . made up his mind that there was room to the north of us for a depot, a town and a speculation. Securing quite a large tract of land at a low price, about $70 an acre, he, with the help of Dr. Kidder, C. L. Jenks and John W. Stewart, all of whom controlled considerable tracts of land in the neighborhood, built a depot, induced the railroad company to make it a stopping place, and the town was begun.[156]

The United States Life Saving Station was built on the lakeshore at the south end of the university campus. The "modern English Gothic" structure was built in 1876-77 by J. B. Consaul of Grand Haven with the work directed by J. L. Parkinson of Evanston. Northwestern had the building demolished in 1954. Photograph by Alexander Hesler.

Real estate began to boom, but some warned that "the prices were inflated and that the bubble would burst."[157] Lots 33 to 50 feet wide, 150 to 180 feet deep, were for sale for $250 to $450 and included sidewalks and shade trees. Culver was selling entire acres for $600 to $1,200 per acre, as well as lending money to build houses. Browne had houses for as little as $1,600; he advertised that he would "take the first payment in lumber, brick, first-class furniture, carpeting, etc., or . . . trade a good family horse and new top buggy, or horses and double carriage for any of the articles named."[158] His lots sold for $7 to $30 a front foot. Browne advertised, "Those wishing to purchase will please take notice that I ornament my lots with Trees and Evergreens, which rapidly enhances their value."[159] He guaranteed that the value of all his property had increased thirty percent over the last five years. He charged eight percent interest, demanding one-fifth in cash, with the rest due in four years.

Grosse Point Lighthouse was designed by O. M. Poe, Major of Engineering, U. S. Army. Work on the tower and keepers' quarters was started in October 1872 and supervised by Evanston resident William F. Bushnell. The light was put into operation by March 1874.

By 1872 this area had its own post office, and a one-room school went up on Central Street at Stewart Avenue. The Methodists built a church at Central Street and Prairie Avenue, which became the center of the social life. Two doctors ministered to the sick: Dr. O. S. Jenks, who reported the successful treatment of "congestive chills and lung fever," and Dr. T. S. Blackburn, who reported "rapid recoveries" for his patients.[160] In February 1873, after three unsuccessful attempts, residents voted 36 to 28 to incorporate the Village of North Evanston and organize a government. Some of those opposed to the village's incorporation filed legal objections, but it took seven months for the judge to make a ruling. In September 1873 the Village of North Evanston finally was able to elect its trustees: Horace C. Fulton, Captain Martin Blackburn, James Goudie, N.W. Boomer, George Foy, and H. C. Parsons.[161]

Meanwhile, on Evanston's southern border another village was in the making:

In 1867 Mr. Gibbs bought from Conrad Schuster 17 acres of land running from Chicago avenue to the lake. On the north-west corner of this tract his house now stands. South Evanston was then only a dream of the future. The next year a station was built and the railroad company induced to stop its trains here, mainly through the efforts of Mr. Gibbs. His house was the only one on the east side of Chicago avenue from Dempster street to Calvary Cemetery. In 1868 he induced Merrill Ladd and Charles B. George to buy the twenty acres adjoining him on the south. They together made the subdivision of Gibbs, Ladd and George's addition to South Evanston, which was the first subdivision made in this village.[162]

Although General Julius White bought eighty acres north of their tract in 1866, it was not platted and recorded until June 1870.[163] In 1871 Warren, Keeney & Company "commenced that series of energetic and well directed operations which have contributed more than anything else to give the place its present enviable status."[164] Judge John B. Adams and Levi C. Pitner developed west of the railroad on the ridge that sold for $15 to $25 a front foot. All these subdivisions platted "at different times and without any effort to harmonize the streets and alleys" made William M. R. Vose suggest that South Evanston "was laid out in the same 'happy go lucky' way that water mains and sewers were laid before Evanston had a municipal system. . . . it always suggested something of man's stupidity, cupidity and pigheadedness."[165] Over the years efforts were made to eliminate the jogs in the streets and alleys where

Evanston and South Evanston met. On January 4, 1873, sixty-seven voters signaled their agreement to incorporate the Village of South Evanston; not one person voted against it. Their incentive to organize a separate village was to escape taxation. Judge John B. Adams was chosen the first president of the board of trustees; with him served A. E. Warren, Thomas H. Watson, Sylvester Goodenow, James S. Kirk, and Collins Shackelford.[166]

Helen Mar Judson Beveridge (1829-1909), the daughter of Philo and Eliza Huddleson Judson, married John Lourie Beveridge in 1848. In April 1854 they moved to Evanston, their home until 1892, except for the four years they spent in Springfield. She headed the Illinois Woman's Centennial Association, which organized a handicraft exhibit for the 1876 Philadelphia Exposition. In 1877 she became one of the incorporators and first president of the Illinois Industrial School for Girls and after she returned to Evanston devoted many years to its charitable work. Photograph by Stickel, Los Angeles.

Fortunes were made and lost in real estate in South Evanston as they were all over the Chicago area. Although there was undoubtedly "stupidity, cupidity and pigheadedness," on the whole, things did not turn out too badly. These subdivisions had attributes important to a fine residential area: lots were large and the streets were wide and tree-lined. However, south Evanston's trustees failed to set aside enough land for parks, nor did they acquire any until many years later. As a result, the area remains limited in park acreage except along the lakefront. School sites were small by present-day standards. In addition to its two public schools, South Evanston also had a home for destitute girls that stood at the foot of Main Street facing the lake. Founded in 1877 by Helen Judson Beveridge, the Illinois Industrial School for Girls provided a home and constructive activities for homeless young women in trouble.[167]

South Evanston's commercial area developed at Chicago Avenue and Lincoln Street, as Main Street was called in the early days. There was an artesian well on Chicago Avenue, where villagers drew their water by hand, whether it was for drinking or to water the saplings that they had set out. This was no small chore, for the trees needed twenty buckets of water a day to survive.[168] No hoses were available, so pails had to be carried back and forth. The village finally built a pumping station to provide drinking water from the lake, but it was only about 600 feet from where the sewer emptied. Because the water was barely drinkable, people continued to draw their water from the artesian well. As the years passed and the population increased, less and less water was available. Little boys sold water in buckets at a nice profit, nor was it uncommon for those on their way to the train in the morning to leave a jug at the well and pick it up when they came home at night. The well water was so hard that people used to make jokes about it.[169]

In February 1874 the *Evanston Index* predicted:

We are looking forward to two notable weddings. One whose silken ties will bind together loving hearts in South Evanston and Evanston. . . . The other anticipated wedding is to be between Evanston and North Evanston. . . . If both vote "aye," the marriage will be consummated and thereafter the two villages will keep house together. Thus one more step will be taken in the plan which is to make the City of Evanston, which is to be one of the most beautiful, flourishing and delightful little cities in the western world. It is only a question of time. It is sure to come, and sooner than many of even the sanguine can now believe.[170]

The first Evanston Waterworks building, designed by Frederick Baumann, was completed in 1875. It stood on the lakeshore on the north side of Lincoln Street. Its construction brought about the annexation of the once separate town of North Evanston, and eventually the issue of pure water would seduce South Evanston to relinquish its independence. Photograph by H. F. Stewart.

The 120-foot tall South Evanston Water tower stood on Chicago Avenue at the west end of Kedzie Street. After South Evanston was annexed to Evanston and began using its water system, the tower was encircled with arc lights whose brilliant glow served as a sailing beacon. It was torn down in 1902 in order to build a new fire station.

In 1874 some North Evanston residents did propose annexation to the Village of Evanston. They used as their arguments the need for a direct road between the North Evanston and the Evanston railroad stations, a thorough system of drainage to connect with the Big Ditch and the lake, and the advantage of the new waterworks. The opponents "based their opposition upon the question of more Taxation, and the fear that they would not be properly represented in our Council, or receive their proportion of expenditures for village purposes." With a vote of 47 to 25, annexation won in the April election.[171] Less than a month later North Evanston residents petitioned their new trustees for a sidewalk on the south side of Lincoln Street. However, almost two decades would pass before South Evanston would give up its autonomy.

Chapter 3

From Village to City

After the Civil War Chicago became the center of the great economic change wrought by the Industrial Revolution. Situated at the heart of the continent, it was the hub of land and water transportation and the nation's third largest manufacturing center. Before the war, merchants, railroads, and small craft industries had dominated the city's economy; afterwards a modern industrial economy—meat packing, printing, iron, steel, lumber, coal, and the garment industry—demanded unskilled labor. The poor of Europe, searching for means of support, flooded into Chicago to fill the demand. Labor formed the Workingman's Party of Illinois during the winter of 1873-74 and the end of the 1870s witnessed almost constant labor unrest.[172] "Down with the aristocrat" became their slogan, and "by 1879 Chicago had become the most important site of socialist activity in the nation."[173]

Lumber merchants like Evanston resident William Blanchard probably agonized during the strike of unskilled Bohemian lumbershovers in May 1876. Evanstonians William Deering and William Hugh Jones must have watched uneasily as strikers moved against their agricultural implement factories. The summer of 1877 brought the great railroad strike. Disorder and rioting in other industries reached such a fever pitch that many middle-class families began to arm themselves. Pressure from the business community finally resulted in Chicago Mayor Monroe Heath's calling out the Illinois National Guard to hold back the battling crowd on Halsted Street. Three thousand strong, the National Guard, the militia, and the police force fought the mob of angry people. Approximately 30 of the workers were killed, 200 wounded, and almost 200 arrested, while only 18 policemen suffered wounds. Evanston must have looked like a haven indeed to the beleaguered factory owners and their associates in the hostile city.[174]

As the financial distress of the 1870s gradually faded, the economy began to prosper with the development of new industries and with the rebuilding of Chicago because of the fire. Men of means, anxious to remove themselves from the threats of angry workers, were moving where open spaces were bigger, wider, and greener, the air cleaner, and where they might have greater control over local government and its services. Evanston, twelve miles north of the city and located on the shore of Lake Michigan, attracted many wealthy families. The university helped create the image of a sedate center of culture free from turmoil. People soon referred to Evanston as the "Athens of the Northwest."[175]

The Northwestern Preparatory School educated most local students for college. For young people from lower-income families public education usually ended at the eighth grade. The little high school that Dr. Otis E. Haven started in 1875 offered only a limited curriculum.[176] There were many in town who looked upon a free public high school as an unnecessary frill, and not until 1882 did Evanstonians vote to establish one.[177] With the passage of a bond issue Evanston Township High School was built at the southeast corner of Dempster Street and Elmwood Avenue and dedicated August 31, 1883. On the first board of trustees were William Blanchard, Sylvester Goodenow, and Shubael D. Childs; they hired as principal Henry L. Boltwood, widely known as the "father of the Township High School in Illinois." A scholar and a leader, Boltwood laid the strong academic foundation during his tenure of twenty-three years that would make Evanston Township High School one of the strongest in the whole country.[178] Ever larger enrollments made several additions to the building necessary. Considerable concern was expressed, however, about the high dropout rate when only twenty-five of the original class of eighty graduated in 1891. Boltwood blamed lack of motivation on the part of the students and parental indifference.[179]

Two other remarkable educators arrived in 1886 to serve as superintendents of two of the elementary systems: Homer H. Kingsley, mathematician and graduate of the University of Michigan, and Frederick W. Nichols, a graduate of Hillsdale College, another Michigan school. Both were dedicated educators and cultured gentlemen who set high standards for their charges and initiated many innovations during their long tenures. Kingsley, who graded the schools, remained superintendent of District 75 for thirty years, and Nichols, who was known as a liberal educator, dominated District 76 for more than half a century.[180] In 1892 Kingsley established a kindergarten at the Wesley Avenue School; Katherine Beebe was the first kindergarten teacher. Public-spirited Irwin Rew and his sister Anna Rew Gross donated money to establish manual training rooms at Haven School, which once stood at the northeast corner of Church Street and Sherman Avenue; they also underwrote the cost of domestic science classrooms.[181]

As the population grew it was necessary to build more schools. In 1892 the board asked Daniel H. Burnham to design a modern building to replace the little two-room school in the Noyes Street neighborhood. By 1894 there were 1,312 children in the central district. Burnham's firm designated another school at Crain Street and Oak Avenue, which was named for the recently deceased Joseph M. Larimer, the school board member responsible for its erection.[182] Four years later Burnham designed another building to replace the original Hinman Avenue School.[183] South Evanston also required new buildings. In 1896 architect John T. Wilson Jennings provided plans for Lincoln School to replace the original building at Judson Avenue and Main Street.[184] Another new building was needed after Central School at the southeast corner of Main Street and Elmwood Avenue was destroyed in a spectacular fire in 1894.[185] There were also enough children in the north end of town in 1894 that the first modest one-room school had to be replaced by a modern brick building, which was later named for school board member Frank P. Crandon.[186]

The first Evanston Township High School was built in 1883 at the southeast corner of Elmwood Avenue and Dempster Street. Designed by Asa Lyon, it was replaced in 1924 by a new building on Dodge Avenue between Church and Lake streets, designed by Perkins Fellows & Hamilton. Henry Leonidas Boltwood (1831-1906) had organized several township high schools in Illinois from 1865 until his appointment as the first principal of Evanston Township High School. In 1891 he was elected president of the State Teachers' Association. Photograph by Fowler.

Frederick W. Nichols (1858-1948), superintendent of District 76 from 1886 to 1943, began his career as a teacher in Michigan, but gained valuable experience as principal and superintendent for various Chicago schools before coming to Evanston. When the school district built the new junior high school on Greenleaf Street in 1928, it was named in his honor.

The 1890s found Evanston women organizing once again to further their children's educational opportunities. Under the guidance of principal Grace Jones Boring, Noyes School parents banded together in the first Mothers' Club, the forerunner of the Parent-Teachers' Association.[187] Women gained the right to vote in school board elections in 1891, which undoubtedly increased their feeling of power. The following year they elected the first woman to a seat on the school board; she was Louise Brockway Stanwood, a civic leader and the second president of the Woman's Club of Evanston.[188]

Civic leaders, ministers, and Northwestern and Garrett professors were all solidly for temperance, working directly for the cause to promote enforcement of the local dry laws. Professors Henry Bannister and David R. Dyche founded the Law and Order League in 1883.[189] Mary Bannister Willard, Frances' sister-in-law, founded a free kindergarten in 1885, which was supported by the Woman's Christian Temperance Union; her motto was "Give us the children until they are six years old and we will risk the rest of their lives."[190] Anna Adams Gordon organized the Loyal Temperance Legion for local children in 1886. African-American women started their own temperance society, which they named in honor of Frances Willard.[191] Through the years, as the zeal in one temperance organization grew weak, someone would start another. Missionary unions in the churches helped the temperance organizations continue their vigorous efforts to keep alcoholic beverages out of Evanston, while they also continued to raise funds to teach and clothe the "heathens" in far-away lands.

Nor did Evanstonians forget their concern for the souls and minds of those they left behind when they fled from the problems in Chicago, the urban poor, the ever-growing mass of illiterate immigrants crowded into dark, city slums south and west of the business district. In 1889 Jane Addams founded Hull-House, the first settlement house in the country, to better conditions for the great influx of people who hoped to find work in American industry. She was a frequent speaker in Evanston and many women followed her example.[192] Elizabeth Eunice Marcy, the wife of Northwestern's first professor of natural science, sold bricks for a dollar apiece outside the Methodist Church to raise money for another settlement house, the Elizabeth E. Marcy Industrial Home.[193] In 1898 Emma Winner Rogers established the Northwestern University Settlement Association with financial help from millionaire Milton Wilson.[194] Mary E. McDowell, who had grown up in Evanston, founded and directed the University of Chicago Settlement.[195] Nor did Evanstonians forget the needy close to home. In 1897 the WCTU established the Delano Settlement in a three-story house at 823 Foster Street to provide wholesome and educational activities for the less fortunate. Christmas baskets were provided for families who needed both food and clothing.[196]

Homer Hitchcock Kingsley (1859-1934) came to Evanston in 1886 upon his appointment as superintendent of District 75, a position he held for thirty years. His wife Nellie Fitch Kingsley (1862-1924), the eldest sister of Lucy Fitch Perkins, was active in many community projects and social organizations; she was one of the organizers of the Community Kitchen, 600 Davis Street. Courtesy Lawrence B. Perkins.

Noyes Street School was constructed in 1892-93 at a cost of $35,000. Built of Racine pressed brick, it was designed by D. H. Burnham & Company. Although the school was closed because of the decline in school-age children, the building continues in service as the Noyes Cultural Arts Center. Photograph by Waterman.

Larimer School, virtually a twin of the Noyes Street School, was built at 1201 Oak Avenue in 1894. Also designed by D. H. Burnham & Company, the building was named for Joseph McMasters Larimer (1851-1894), the school board member most responsible for its erection. The building was razed in 1936 and the site dedicated as Larimer Park.
Photograph by Charles R. Childs.

In 1898 the Hinman Avenue School designed by Asa Lyon in 1883 was replaced by a new structure designed by D. H. Burnham & Company. In 1910 it was renamed for Humphreys Henry Clay Miller (1845-1910), president of the District 75 School Board from 1891 until he died. Miller, who lived at 1707 Hinman Avenue, also served as president of the Evanston board of trustees from 1888 to 1890 and as second vice president of the Northwestern board of trustees from 1896 to 1910. The building now houses the Chiaravalle Montessori School.

Lincoln School, architect John T. Wilson Jennings' masterpiece in Evanston, was built in 1896. After seventy-two years of service, the ornate structure at the northwest corner of Main Street and Forest Avenue gave way to the wrecker's ball. Two of the terra cotta gargoyles that graced the façade have been preserved by the Evanston History Center. Photograph by Hartwell.

When South Evanston's Central School on the southeast corner of Main Street and Elmwood Avenue was destroyed by fire in March 1894, it was replaced the following January by a new structure. Designed by Thomas & Rapp, the second Central School survived until 1960. Photograph by Chandler.

Central Street School, 2108 Central Street, was built in 1894 by William C. Pocklington. Renamed for former school board member Frank Philip Crandon (1834-1919) several years after his death, Crandon School was demolished in 1931.
Photograph by Charles R. Childs.

Elizabeth Eunice Smith Marcy (1821-1911), the wife of Professor Oliver Marcy, was one of the founders of the Woman's Christian Temperance Union, active in missionary societies and the Daughters of the American Revolution, as well as the author of poems, hymns, and Facts and Fancies of Family History. A settlement home in Chicago at Maxwell and Newberry streets, named in her honor, opened in March 1896.
Photograph by Charles E. Smith.

But there were few facilities to cope with illness, only a small pesthouse in which to isolate smallpox victims. Typhoid fever and the serious children's diseases, diphtheria and scarlet fever, hit at one time or another almost every family. Nor did disease respect family fortune. Susan Pratt Leonhardt, who had been the first non-Native American baby born in the Grosse Pointe settlement, in three weeks lost four of her children during a particularly virulent epidemic in 1880.[197] Consumption carried off many a young adult. And complications during childbirth lost many a new mother. During the extremely cold winter of 1883 a baby froze to death. This tragedy inspired Sarah B. Blanchard, the wife of the prominent lumber merchant William Blanchard, to gather friends at her Italianate villa at 1608 Ridge Avenue to organize the Benevolent Society of Evanston.[198]

Susan Pratt Leonhardt (1840-1910), the first child born to any of the settlers in Grosse Pointe, married coal dealer Louis Leonhardt in 1857. With their family of twelve children, they made their home at 1944 Ridge Avenue, which was demolished in 1929.
Photograph by Alexander Hesler.

In this "paradise for women,"[199] three women doctors joined male members of their profession as successful practitioners—Dr. Sarah H. Brayton came in 1883;[200] Dr. Mary F. McCrillis, a homeopathic physician, arrived in 1888;[201] and in 1889 Dr. Harriet Wolf settled in South Evanston.[202] As early as 1874 there was a board of health.[203] Pasteur's discovery of the germ theory in 1877 and new immunization techniques helped reduce the disease toll. In 1892 the Visiting Nurse Association began to meet the health needs of the poor and aid in the prevention of the spread of infectious diseases.[204] That same year a hospital was finally established in a modest frame house at 806 Emerson Street. In 1898 the first permanent Evanston Hospital building would open on Ridge Avenue north of Central Street.[205]

Evanston Hospital's first permanent building, 2650 Ridge Avenue, was the culmination of several years of planning; although the site and the architect, George Lyons Harvey, were chosen in 1895, the building was not completed until 1898.

In 1878 a local dentist, Dr. Charles A. Garnsey, and a Northwestern professor of physics and chemistry, Henry Smith Carhart, announced improvements to Alexander Graham Bell's telephone, which had been invented two years before.[206] The first telephone exchange was set up in 1882 in Dr. Garnsey's office at 610 Davis Street.[207] In 1887 the post office began free mail delivery. As a result street numbers had to be assigned to the houses.[208]

The 1880s saw the formation of clubs to promote culture throughout the United States; Evanston was no exception. Among the clubs that met in Evanston's spacious homes was the Legensia, organized January 30, 1880, for literary exercises: "The flippant never entered into its discussions, and even the discussion of the protective tariff never precipitated any lifelong animosities."[209] The Bryant Circle was organized in 1885; open only to women, its members prepared papers on all manner of cultural subjects.[210] Some of the clubs were more social and less intellectual than those of an earlier day.

The Shingle Style clubhouse of the Evanston Club, designed by Holabird & Roche, was built on the northwest corner of Grove Street and Chicago Avenue. The grand opening was held on October 1, 1889, and the building was a familiar and beloved sight until its demise in 1958 after sitting vacant for two years.

After railroad executive Marshall M. Kirkman organized the Evanston Country Club in 1888, it became the center of social life for the well-to-do.[211] Evanston's most prominent men organized the Evanston Club the same year; for men only, the club had Kirkman at its head too. Holabird & Roche designed its large shingled clubhouse that once stood on the northwest corner of Grove Street and Chicago Avenue.[212]

Marshall Monroe Kirkman (1842-1921), a novelist and author of many books on railroads, served as vice president of the Chicago North Western Railroad from 1889 to 1910. Founder and first president of both the Evanston Country Club and the Evanston Club, he was voted the most prominent Evanstonian in a contest held by the Evanston Press in 1891. In 1921 he donated part of his large estate "Larchmere" to the Country Club for its tennis courts; in 1944 the site became Merrick Park and four years later it was dedicated as Merrick Rose Garden. Photograph by Fowler.

The Evanston Country Club, designed by Holabird & Roche, was completed in 1892. Although this center of Evanston social life was destroyed by fire in December 1922, the membership rallied to plan a new building; it opened for a gala New Year's Eve the following year. In 1946 the second clubhouse was converted into City Hall and under this guise survived until 1979. Photograph from Classic Evanston.

Most ambitious of all the organizations was the Woman's Club of Evanston, formed in an era when women were organizing to pursue their interests and become more effective in their homes and communities. This new club combined cultural and social aspects with philanthropy. Its organizer and first president, Elizabeth Boynton Harbert, was one of the leaders in the struggle for women's rights in Illinois. For seven years she edited the "Woman's Kingdom," a column in the *Chicago Inter Ocean*. In January 1885 she bought the weekly journal *Our Herald* and changed its name to the *New Era*, but had to discontinue publishing it by December because she was so overworked. From the time of her arrival in Evanston in 1874, her large home at 1412 Judson Avenue was Evanston's literary salon. Among the notable American authors and thinkers who spoke there was Bronson Alcott. After she organized the Woman's Club in 1889 she opened her home to the club's manifold activities.[213]

Author, lecturer, philanthropist, and foremost advocate of woman's suffrage, Elizabeth Boynton Harbert (1845-1925) came to Evanston in 1874 with her husband William S. Harbert. She was the founder and first president of the Woman's Club of Evanston.

At the end of the nineteenth century there was an outburst of creative activity and in Chicago a cultural renaissance was in the making—writers, composers, and architects were seeking new ideas. Musicians had banded together in 1882 in the Evanston Amateur Musical Club, founded by Cornelia Gray Lunt, the artistically-inclined and civic-minded daughter of Orrington Lunt. The Thomas Concert Class was started in October 1896, made up of subscribers to the Chicago Symphony Orchestra, conducted by Theodore Thomas.[214] In 1897 the Woman's Club added a Music Department and the dynamic Sadie Knowland Coe served as its director. For the 1899-1900 season she devoted the programs exclusively to women composers; American composers were the theme for the following year.[215]

Sculptor Lorado Taft lived in Evanston from 1889 to 1898. A lecturer at the Art Institute of Chicago, he gave a series of talks in Evanston at the high school to promote interest in the arts: "historically and artistically the lectures were a success—financially a failure," because attendance did not live up to expectations.[216]

Evanstonians watched with interest the Broadway success of Kathryn Kidder who played the role of Dearest in *Little Lord Fauntleroy,* as well as starring roles in *Held by the Enemy* and *The Leavenworth Case.* Her greatest triumph was playing a Parisian laundress, who became a duchess matching wits with Emperor Napoleon Bonaparte, in Victorien Sardou's and Émile Moreau's drama, *Madame Sans-Gêne.* By opening night in January 1895 the theater had been sold out a month in advance.[217] Following an Evanston-raised daughter's glamorous career undoubtedly spurred interest in the theater in Evanston.

Kathryn Kidder (1869-1939), the granddaughter of Daniel Parish Kidder and Harriet Kidder, began her acting career in 1885 in the role of Lucy Fairweather in "The Streets of New York". Married to the playwright Louis Anspacher, she became a famous actress and starred in Shakespearean tragedies and French romantic comedies alike. Photograph by W. J. Root.

On the lighter side, William C. "Deacon" Garwood added to Evanston's claim to fame when he introduced the ice cream soda and curb service to the town at his drugstore on Fountain Square. There are those who also credit Evanston with the invention of the ice cream sundae: "never on Sunday" applied to many a leisure activity in this "sanctified" town. To absolve the sin of sipping an ice cream soda on Sunday, the ice cream and syrup were served without the scintillating soda water. Its name was changed to "sundae" because some felt calling it a "Sunday" was sacrilegious.[218]

Garwood's Drug Store supplanted Colvin's Store on the northeast corner of Davis Street and Orrington Avenue. William C. "Deacon" Garwood (1852-1938) also opened a branch in 1890 in the Orr Block on the southwest corner of Dempster Street and Chicago Avenue.

In 1887 Northwestern's science department moved into Fayerweather Hall. Designed by Holabird & Roche, it stood at the head of Hinman Avenue until 1954. The site, now marked with a plaque, lay between Kresge Centennial Hall and the dormitories built close to Sheridan Road. Photograph by P. B. Green.

The university's growth paralleled that of the town. Professors were said to be "as common as swallows, and sometimes as flitting and as flippant."[219] Northwestern boasted the first building in Chicago or its suburbs erected especially for instruction in the sciences—Fayerweather Hall designed by Holabird & Roche and built in 1886-87.[220] When Dearborn Observatory, designed by Cobb & Frost, was completed in 1889, the university established the astronomy department with George Washington Hough as its distinguished director.[221] For the 1890-91 term 383 students were enrolled in the college and 692 in the preparatory school, while Evanston's population had reached 13,059.[222] In 1890 the Northwestern board departed from its precedent of selecting a Methodist minister as president and elected Henry Wade Rogers, dean of the University of Michigan Law School, to succeed Joseph Cummings who had died of a heart attack.[223] His wife Emma Winner Rogers became an outstanding leader during their ten-year residence here. In 1892 she took a step towards improving the relationship between Northwestern and Evanston by bringing together representatives of each in the formation of the University Guild.[224]

Cornelia Gray Lunt was instrumental in bringing Peter Christian Lutkin, the organist at St. James Episcopal Church in Chicago, to reorganize Northwestern's music department, chaotic since the resignation of Oren Locke in 1891.[225] It was one of the first music schools associated with a university in the United States. Lutkin wished to give music students a well-rounded cultural education in the proper atmosphere because he felt that:

> *In large cities there is, unhappily, a tinge of the moral laxity prevalent in European capitals among professional men. . . . the wholesome surroundings of Evanston offer a marked contrast. Its churches and Christian associations, its freedom from saloons and questionable resorts, together with its educational facilities and attractive location, make it an ideal home for the pursuit of a musical education. Evanston, with its beautiful homes and cultured residents, should take a peculiar pride in the cultivation of the fine arts, and should support all educational efforts in that direction.* [226]

Lutkin brought other stars of the musical world to his department: Arne Oldberg and Sadie Knowland Coe both joined the faculty as piano instructors.[227] In 1898 the Music School moved into its own building at 716-22 University Place; designed by William A. Otis, it was "an abode where [the music students] were free to propagate as many sound waves as [they] wished without disturbing the liberal arts students."[228]

Northwestern's departments were expanding. The noted elocutionist Robert McLean Cumnock had established the School of Oratory in 1878. Meat packer Gustavus Franklin Swift and his wife, Ann Higgins Swift, donated money for a building in memory of their daughter who had been one of the Cumnock's students. In 1894 a site was selected and the following year Annie May Swift Hall, designed by Charles Robert Ayars, was dedicated, the only building devoted to a speech school at the time anywhere in the world.[229]

Organist, composer, and first dean of Northwestern's School of Music, Peter Christian Lutkin (1858-1931) came to Evanston in 1892. Active in organizing the Evanston Musical Club as well as the University Glee Club, Lutkin did not live to see the construction of the performance hall erected in his honor. Photograph by J. D. Toloff.

Dearborn Observatory, named in honor of Mary Dearborn Scammon, was completed in June 1889. The Richardsonian Romanesque structure designed by Cobb & Frost was built to house a telescope that, at the time, had the world's largest lens. When the Technological Institute was contemplated in 1939, the observatory was moved closer to the lake and now is nestled behind Garrett Biblical Institute and the Shakespeare Garden.

Annie May Swift Hall was built 1894-95 for the School of Oratory. It was one of the first independent commissions of architect Charles Robert Ayars, the son of James Ayars (1836-1893), president of the Evanston board of trustees from 1885 to 1888.

Robert McLean Cumnock (1840-1928) joined the Northwestern faculty in 1868. Ten years later he established the School of Oratory, the predecessor of the School of Speech. Author of Choice Readings, Cumnock lived at 1804 Hinman Avenue from 1887 until 1917; the house burned down in 1970.

In 1892 the university decided to build a library. It was completed in 1894, almost forty years after the first Northwestern building went up on the corner of Davis Street and Hinman Avenue. The neo-classical building designed by William A. Otis was named for Orrington Lunt, the major benefactor.[230] In 1896 William Deering gave the university $215,000, the largest gift it had yet received; it was used partly to build Fisk Hall, designed by Daniel H. Burnham, to house the ever-expanding preparatory school. Deering became president of the board of trustees in 1897, a post he held until 1906.[231]

The Village of South Evanston had first proposed joining Evanston in 1883 in order to enjoy the benefits of the municipal water supply. Residents of both villages proposed giving up the village form of government if the two were to merge. There were plenty of citizens, however, who shied at the thought of giving up the separate identity of each, not to mention the idea of Evanston's becoming a city. "City" was a dirty word: *The Nickel's Worth* described South Evanston as a town that was:

Out of the grime and the grind of the great city so far as to be possessed of a goodly country atmosphere, and where there is so much of it that every one can appropriate a share for himself without being obliged to select that which has previously done duty for various other mortals. It is so far removed from the conditions of the city as to escape that crowding of gas mains and sewer pipes which causes a greater emission of noxious odors than the atmosphere can bear without serious contaminations. . . . Nerve-strained men and women of the city will never realize the rest that comes from even a momentary communion with nature until they cut loose from the confinement of their bastile homes and drink anew of the serenity and soothing pure air and plenty of elbow room.[232]

Alexander Clark,[233] a proponent of annexation and city status tried to win converts by saying:

Calling a city of ten or fifteen thousand a village, don't make it any more rural. It simply combines the worst elements of both. A city organization does not necessarily imply ward strikers and bummers. It only enables every neighborhood to get a representation. I admit that calling a man an alderman may be pretty hard on him, but self-sacrificing men will be found in Evanston who will shoulder this odium for the public good. A mayor and common council need be no more costly than a president and board of trustees. If men can be found to serve on the one without compensation, they can on the other.[234]

The referendum took place on February 20, 1892, after "a hard fought campaign" that "marshaled every possible voter."[235] The men of Evanston cast 851 votes for annexation, 444 against. In South Evanston the tally showed 334 in favor, 250 against the proposition. On election night a mammoth bonfire illuminated Fountain Square and the streets echoed with the music of tin horns and serenades by the Ravenswood Brass Band.[236]

After the hubbub and furor over annexation subsided, the City of Evanston held an election that April for mayor and fourteen aldermen. No voter's registration existed at that time and all kinds of irregularities took place: there was "good reason to believe that a large illegal student vote was cast," as well as voting by "parties not residents of the city." The *Evanston Press* reprimanded "At no election held in this township were ever heard so many charges of collusion, fraud, the use of money, and the use of those electioneering adjuncts which are the concomitants of elections of non-temperance towns." Among those challenged, however, was former Governor John L. Beveridge, the son-in-law of Philo Judson, Civil War general, and a distinguished resident of Evanston for thirty years.[237]

Dr. Oscar H. Mann won the mayoralty by only a very narrow margin and the results of the aldermanic race in one ward remained in doubt so there had to be a recount. The *Evanston Press* admonished that voting irregularities "are likely to be considered by our neighbors as a reflection upon the boasted intelligence of a city whose judges of election through undue haste and non observance of the laws create confusion in its first civic election."[238] When the Village of Hyde Park was annexed to

Chicago in 1889 and the Village of Rogers Park in 1893, there were those who proposed that Evanston was also ripe for annexation.[239] However, the people who wished to remain independent and keep the simpler, rural ambiance of the town won in the election held in April 1894. There were 2,155 who voted against becoming a part of Chicago, while only 642 were in favor.[240]

Orrington Lunt Library, which formally opened in 1894, established William A. Otis' reputation as a designer of libraries. The building, which also housed the rooms of the University Guild, served as the library until 1932. After Deering Library opened, Lunt was adapted to administrative and classroom use, and it even served as a naval barracks during World War II.

Named in honor of Herbert Franklin Fisk (1840-1916), principal of the Northwestern Preparatory School for thirty-one years, Fisk Hall opened in January 1899. Designed by D. H. Burnham & Company, it housed the Preparatory School until 1917 when it was taken over by the College of Liberal Arts. Since 1954 Fisk has been the home of the Joseph Medill School of Journalism.

Dr. Oscar H. Mann (1834-1911) came to Evanston in 1867 with his wife Amanda Fitch Mann. President in 1871 of the Cook County Medical Society and in 1872 of the Illinois State Medical Society, Dr. Mann served on Evanston's board of health and on the village board of trustees. When Evanston was incorporated as a city in 1892, he was elected the first mayor.

The newly elected city council was, as ever, concerned about streets. The issue on the community agenda the longest was the matter of a good road along the lakeshore. About 1887 civic agitation to pave this road all the way from Chicago to Milwaukee and create a beautiful boulevard along which people might enjoy driving their carriages culminated in the formation of the Sheridan Road Improvement Association by Evanstonian Volney W. Foster. Each town would be responsible for its own share, although quality of the upkeep would vary over the years.[241] It would take more than twenty-five years of political maneuvering, civic debate, and laws passed by the state legislature for Sheridan Road finally to be paved all the way to Milwaukee.

At the beginning almost no one foresaw the mass production and use of the automobile, which would later cause the road to become rutted and difficult to negotiate. However, on Thanksgiving Day, 1895, Evanstonians witnessed the nation's first automobile race. Six "motocycles" began the race; only two finished the fifty-four-mile course from Chicago's Jackson Park to Evanston and back. The two-cylinder automobile designed and built by J. Frank Duryea won. Two years later Dr. Edward Webster purchased the first automobile in Evanston, a one-cylinder Cadillac.[242]

There were new public conveniences, especially in transportation. In the 1890s the growing population and new developments resulted in agitation for better transportation to and from Chicago and within Evanston itself. Long debate began in 1892-93 over a franchise for a street railway system from Chicago to Evanston. Strong opposition came from those who "claimed that the reason they moved [to Evanston] was to get out in the country and away from street cars."[243] The proponents won, however, and the Chicago North Shore Street Railway Company received its franchise. With several transfers one could ride north from Irving Park Boulevard in Chicago as far as Emerson Street in Evanston. Some of the promoters of the street railway were also interested in Evanston real estate, among them Charles Yerkes, the acknowledged "boss" of Chicago's street railway system, who had subdivided land near

Sherman Avenue and Central Street.[244] Because of these pressures the street cars soon reached Central Street; then they turned west and continued to Bennett Avenue, where there was a public park, very popular with picnickers during the summer. Later the trolley line on Central Street was extended two blocks to the city limits at Lincolnwood Drive where one could transfer to the North Shore & Western Railway, which was organized in 1906 by lawyer George P. Merrick. At Lincolnwood Drive the route went south to Harrison Street where the line went west to the new Glenview Golf Club, of which Merrick was a member. A "blind pig," or illegal saloon, in Harms Woods north of the trestle over the Chicago River and Memorial Park Cemetery brought two other sorts of patrons to the railway, known locally as the "Toonerville Trolley" or the "Dinkey."[245]

Although there were those who poked fun at the quiet village that they called "Hevanston,"[246] people who wanted quiet and fresh air were willing to overlook such smugness. Men of wealth continued to buy large lots, usually on Ridge and Asbury avenues, or on streets close to the lake, Forest, Michigan, and Judson avenues. Land values began to rise again. In 1882 Mrs. James F. White paid $5,500 for a 95' by 100' lot at Greenwood Street and Hinman Avenue; W. L. Randall bought a 66' by 200' lot on Hinman Avenue for $3,300; and George M. Sargent paid $3,600 for a 66' by 200' lot at the northwest corner of Hinman Avenue and Grove Street.[247] While local tradespeople and those of modest means hired carpenters and contractors to build simple, but comfortable houses, often copied from the old pattern books, the wealthy demanded the services of architects. Architecture became a recognized profession as colleges began to offer instruction; the first two in the country were the Massachusetts Institute of Technology in Cambridge and the University of Illinois in Champaign. Until they were established, would-be architects, like would-be doctors and lawyers, learned their profession apprenticed to experienced professionals. A year at the prestigious Ecole des Beaux Arts in Paris would often complete the education of an aspiring architect. A few women were even entering the new profession.

Commission merchant Nelson B. Record hired Asa Lyon, Evanston's first resident architect, to design his home at 1454 Asbury Avenue. Built 1881-82, it is one of three houses by Lyon that remain virtually unchanged more than a century later. Photograph by Jenny Thompson.

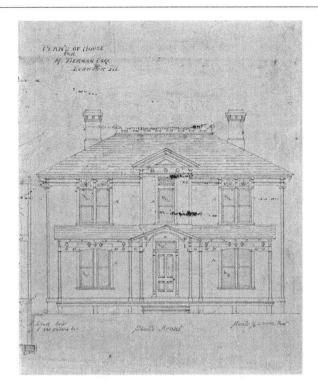

The Michael and Mary Stockton Tiernan house, 215 Lake Street, is another of the houses by Asa Lyon. Completed in December 1881, the house underwent a 1983 restoration of its exterior with the benefit of a complete set of original plans preserved in the Evanston History Center.

When construction resumed in the 1880s Gothic and Italianate architecture had lost favor. One of the new styles came to be known as the stick style because the framing members were articulated on the exterior and were part of the final visual effect. Large verandas with posts and braces amplified the stick construction.[248] Asa Lyon, generally considered Evanston's first resident architect, designed several houses in this style. Lyon lived in South Evanston from 1872 to 1875, but moved back into Chicago for several years as he tried to survive the dearth of construction after the financial panic of 1873. When he returned to Evanston in 1881, his services were "in great demand" and he advertised that he would try to "study the interests of his clients in all cases."[249] He adapted ideas from current architectural magazines and designed houses that cost from $3,500 to $10,000.[250] Among Lyon's extant works are the house at 1314 Hinman Avenue, designed in 1882 for Eunice Clarinda Reed, the widow of banker Asa D. Reed; one at 1454 Asbury Avenue for commission merchant Nelson B. Record; and another at 215 Lake Street for Michael Tiernan.

Houses of the 1880s and 1890s had interiors more spacious than those built in the 1860s and 1870s. Under the influence of the English architect Richard Norman Shaw and the Boston architect Henry Hobson Richardson, the entrance hall had evolved into a reception room, or living hall, that featured a handsome fireplace and a monumental stair. Tiles, often imported from Europe, ornamented the fireplace and testified to the owner's taste. The improvement of central heating made large houses with more open interior spaces possible. The word "picturesque" described houses in the Queen Anne style whose exteriors were elaborate and busy with towers, cupolas, bays, and verandas.

Chicago architect Cass Chapman designed John Hume Kedzie's spacious residence that once stood at 1514 Ridge Avenue. Fire, a constant threat, had destroyed Kedzie's first two houses on the same site. The third house, built in 1881, was sheathed in cream brick and had wide verandas stretching across the front and halfway on the sides; an observatory tower was said to rise eight-four feet. A very "neat and tasty" black walnut staircase led to the second floor, which contained six large bedrooms. A marble floor in the vestibule and stained glass windows added to the luxury.[251] In 1882 John Evans sold his block of lakefront property to Lemuel D. Norton for $25,000, one of the largest real estate deals thus far.[252] The $20,000 house that Norton commissioned Chicago architect Edward Baumann to design contained twenty rooms, twelve closets, a long porch, a tower, and even a conservatory. "Modern Renaissance" in style, it was considered "the finest residence yet built in a suburb, even in as fine a place as Evanston."[253] Another large Queen Anne house was built in 1883 for lawyer Curtis H. Remy facing the lake at 1622 Forest Place. It featured a large veranda, a cherry-paneled frieze in the dining room, and tiles with the story of Little Red Riding Hood in the nursery.[254]

Cass Chapman, architect of the First Baptist Church and the second First Methodist Church, also designed the third house of John Hume Kedzie (1815-1903), 1514 Ridge Avenue, in 1881. Involved in real estate in South Evanston and Ravenswood, Kedzie was among those at the meeting at which the Republican Party in Illinois was organized. He also served four years as the first president of the Free Public Library, which was established in 1873, and in 1876 he was elected to the Illinois legislature. The house was demolished in 1967 for a parking lot that was subsequently redeveloped at St. Mark's Court.

Architects competed to design the houses of the well-to-do. The Chicago merchant Simeon Farwell chose John Mills Van Osdel, Chicago's first architect, to design his turreted Queen Anne mansion at 1433 Hinman Avenue in 1890. Van Osdel came to Chicago from New York in 1837 to design the home of William B. Ogden, Chicago's first mayor. Van Osdel went on to win the respect of Chicago's building industry. In 1890 he was approaching the end of his long and vigorous life. His nephew, John Mills Van Osdel II, who carried on his uncle's firm, probably had more to do with carrying out Farwell's wishes. The elaborate plaster ornamentation, or parget work, in the gable was new to Evanston, and the Farwell house is unique in Evanston.[255]

On the site of John Evans' home, architect Edward Baumann designed a twenty-room mansion for Lemuel D. and Mary E. Norton. Completed in 1882, the $20,000 house at 1800 Sheridan Road was totally transformed by the remodeling by Ernest A. Mayo in 1916. On this venerable site, the building continues to serve as Northwestern's John Evans Alumni Center.

One of the most striking Queen Anne houses in Evanston was one of the last works of John Mills Van Osdel. Built in 1890 for Simeon Farwell (1831-1911) and his wife Ebenette Smith Farwell, the house at 1433 Hinman Avenue features pressed brick, elaborate parget work, and a panoply of towers and bays. Photograph by Jenny Thompson.

Stephen A. Jennings came to Evanston in 1885, a year after Asa Lyon left for greener pastures, and succeeded him as the most fashionable architect. A graduate of the University of Illinois, he was well-versed in the vagaries of the Queen Anne style and glib of tongue in persuading his clients that they needed a picturesque castle, whether of wood, brick or stone.[256]

One of Jennings' best known wooden castles was built at 1560 Oak Avenue in 1892 for John W. and Jennie Low. It was said that she later complained that Jennings had designed a house more elaborate than they really desired. The Low house featured a conical tower with a dunce-cap roof, which became a Jennings cliché, and a Palladian window, one of the hallmarks of the Queen Anne vocabulary. The exterior reflected the interior plan and produced interesting facades on all sides, although the fenestration seemed somewhat disorganized.[257] In 1919, the house became the headquarters of the Catholic Woman's Club. In the 1970s, the building was identified as an historic landmark. It was purchased in 2007. In 2011, the house was being remodeled, with plans for turning it into a clock museum, when it caught fire and was severely damaged. The ruins of the house were then razed.

When his client could afford it, Jennings used large rock-faced stone as Henry Hobson Richardson so often had done. Perhaps Jennings' masterpiece and certainly the most costly of his residential designs is the mansion at 1232 Ridge Avenue built for the agricultural implement manufacturer William Hugh Jones in 1894-95. Jennings used grey granite on the exterior and designed a mammoth fireplace using the same stone. One of the house's most spectacular features is the monumental stair, which had a Lyon & Healy organ installed on the first landing.[258] St. Mary's Roman Catholic Church, another of Jennings' achievements, was built in 1891-92 at a cost of $45,000.[259] William C. Pocklington, who learned the building trade in Waukegan and came to Evanston in 1871, helped proliferate the Queen Anne style. He was a carpenter and contractor, but called himself an architect despite no formal training.[260]

Stephen A. Jennings' masterpiece in Evanston is the twenty-room granite mansion that he designed for William Hugh Jones (1845-1916), 1232 Ridge Avenue. Involved in the agricultural implement business since 1866, Jones was named vice president of the conglomerate International Harvester when it was organized in 1902. Photograph from Classic Evanston.

St. Mary's Roman Catholic Church, built of Lemont limestone in 1891-92, was also designed by Stephen A. Jennings, who was a parishioner. The two 100-foot-tall spires were copied from St. Patrick's Church in Philadelphia.

In the last phase of the Queen Anne, shingles sheathed the upper story, sometimes the whole house. The Shingle Style, brought to prominence by the work of Boston architect Henry Hobson Richardson, emphasized the surface and its texture rather than the skeletal frame; it introduced the concept of the open plan and moved toward an integration of interior and exterior space:

In sum, the American house had now undergone a variety of changes adapting it to American conditions, functional requirements, and materials. . . . The openness and flow of its space are American. So are the sheltering void of the piazza, the lightly scaled woodwork, and the rough shingles. . . . That it should be called American has nothing to do with chauvinistic enthusiasms. . . . The term signifies a sensitive adjustment of materials, techniques, and sense of space to specific and newly evaluated condition of American living.[261]

Evanston has some fine examples of the Shingle Style: the house at 1501 Forest Avenue that the firm of Handy & Cady designed for Frank M. and Anna Shuman Elliot in 1887 is "a beautiful example of Romanesque features of the Queen Anne without any of its barbarisms."[262] The elaborate house at 1144 Michigan Avenue was designed in 1890 by Enoch Hill Turnock, who had worked for William LeBaron Jenney, for Charles Jernegan, a member of the Board of Trade,[263] while that at 1232 Asbury Avenue was designed for coal merchant Clement Knowles Pittman in 1891 by William Augustus Otis, Jenney's former partner.[264] One of the latest houses in this style was built in 1896-97 at 1228 Forest Avenue and designed by Franklin P. Burnham for William H. Burnet.[265]

Although the majority of Evanston residences were designed by Evanston and Chicago architects, the grandest of this period is the work of an "alien," the New York architect Henry Edwards-Ficken. The home of the Evanston History Center since 1960, the twenty-eight room mansion at 225 Greenwood Street was built in 1894-95 for Robert D. Sheppard. An ordained minister, a professor of political science, and Northwestern's treasurer and business manager, Sheppard hoped to become president of the university. Edwards-Ficken borrowed heavily from the design of Chambord, one of the most famous French chateaux in the Loire Valley. Although Edwards-Ficken designed other houses in the East in the Jacobean style, Sheppard probably felt a French chateau more in keeping with his anticipated status. However, he lost the presidency by one vote of the board of trustees. Financial difficulties made his enjoyment of the house short-lived. In 1909 Charles Gates Dawes purchased the house for $75,000 and it remained his home until his death in 1951. Brigadier General during World War I, Dawes was the first Director of the United States Bureau of the Budget. He served as Vice President of the United States from 1925 to 1929 under President Calvin Coolidge and shared the Nobel Peace Prize for 1925 with Sir Austen Chamberlain, the British Foreign Secretary. From 1929 to 1932 he was the Ambassador to Great Britain.[266]

The residence of Frank Micajah Elliot (1853-1919) and his wife Anna Shuman Elliot on the northeast corner of Forest Avenue and Lake Street was designed by Handy & Cady. Built in 1887, it is a superb example of a Shingle Style. Photograph by Jenny Thompson.

Another imposing Shingle Style house at 1144 Michigan Avenue was built in 1890 for Charles and Elizabeth Jernegan. Architect Enoch Hill Turnock accentuated the swells of bays and turrets by a skin of shingles that sheathes the upper stories, which seem to hover over and shelter the lower story. Photograph by Jenny Thompson.

The home of Clement Knowles and Georgia Greene Pittman, 1232 Asbury Avenue, has a complicated system of roofs and shingled gables that loom over the clapboard-covered first floor. Designed by William A. Otis, it was built in 1891-92. Photograph by Jenny Thompson.

Franklin P. Burnham was the architect of the William H. Burnet house, 1228 Forest Avenue. Built in 1896-97, it was the home of Charles Gates Dawes from 1904 to 1909. As the Queen Anne and Shingle styles waned, more and more classical details were introduced, and this house with its dentils, columns, and Palladian windows shows this increased classical influence. Photograph by Jenny Thompson.

A number of architects came here to live, attracted by the large number of wealthy, potential clients. Two of Chicago's most famous architects chose Evanston as their home. William Holabird moved to Evanston in the 1880s and designed his family's home at 1500 Oak Avenue.[267] His firm, Holabird & Roche, became nationally famous for its innovative construction techniques for skyscrapers in Chicago. They designed several residences in Evanston, as well as the Evanston Club and the lovely City Hall that once stood at the northwest corner of Fountain Square. Daniel Hudson Burnham moved to Evanston in 1887; he bought Robert M. Hatfield's twenty-room grout house on Forest Avenue; the house and spacious grounds that extended to the lake were testimony to his wealth and power.[268] One of Evanston's prominent and respected citizens, he headed Chicago's most powerful architectural firm and was the first Evanstonian elected national president of the American Institute of Architects.[269] With his partner, the gifted designer John Wellborn Root, Burnham created a number of large homes in Evanston.[270] Of those that remain, only one is little altered, the large brick house at 1462 Ridge Avenue that was built in 1883 for George Watson Smith, who married John Hume Kedzie's daughter.[271] One of the last designs of this partnership before Root's untimely death in 1892 was Emmanuel Methodist Episcopal Church, perhaps the best example in Evanston of the influence of architect Henry Hobson Richardson.[272]

Charles Gates Dawes (1865-1951), lawyer, banker, author, composer, and philanthropist, served as vice president under President Calvin Coolidge from 1925 to 1929. Dawes deeded his house to Northwestern in the hope that the Evanston Historical Society (now known as the Evanston History Center) would one day establish a museum in his home. In 2009, Northwestern University donated the house to the Evanston History Center.

Built in 1894-96 for Robert Dickinson Sheppard, treasurer and business manager of Northwestern University, the Chateauesque Style lakefront mansion, 225 Greenwood Street, is better known as the home of Charles Gates Dawes. Since 1960 the house has served as the headquarters of the Evanston History Center. In 1982, the house and grounds underwent a major renovation. Another extensive restoration and preservation project, which includes the rebuilding of the house's conservatory, was launched in 2011. Photograph by Jenny Thompson.

One of the smaller masterpieces of the giant architectural firm of Burnham & Root is the Emmanuel Methodist Church on the northeast corner of Oak Avenue and Greenwood Street. Built 1890-92, "the petted daughter of the wealthy First Methodist Church," was constructed of red Ashland stone at a cost of $60,000. Photograph by Jenny Thompson.

Burnham masterminded the major event of the 1890s—the 1893 World's Columbian Exposition. Another Evanstonian, banker Lyman Gage, was the fair's chairman and many others played a role in its creation and operation. Most of the major buildings of the "Great White City" were designed in a neo-classical style by some of the illustrious architects of the eastern seaboard. But the real architectural lesson of the fair was the impact of buildings arranged in support of each other. Burnham's concept of the fair's plan would survive in his plans for cities both here and abroad, which established his reputation as the "father of city planning."[273] However, it was the neo-classical style of most of the buildings that people who went to the fair remembered, which made Louis Sullivan declare, "the damage wrought by the World's Fair will last for half a century from its date, if not longer. It has penetrated deep into the constitution of the American mind, effecting there lesions significant of dementia."[274] The fair certainly had its impact on Evanston as those who wanted to be in fashion demanded porticoes of Corinthian columns and elaborate pediments added to their houses. The fair also ushered in a period of classicism, revivalism, and eclecticism. But just beyond the turn of the century was a new generation of architects ready to rethink the design of the American house.

Holabird & Roche was one of the three most prominent architectural firms of the Chicago School. William Holabird (1854-1912) came to Chicago in 1875 and worked in the office of William LeBaron Jenney. During the first years of independent practice, Holabird moved to Evanston and ca. 1882-83 built his home at 1500 Oak Avenue. It was razed in 1969.

Completion of the City Hall on the northwest corner of Fountain Square in 1892 soon after Evanston's incorporation as a city marked the beginning of a new phase in Evanston's political life. The building, designed by Holabird & Roche, also housed the public library.

Architect and planner Daniel Hudson Burnham (1846-1912) lived in Evanston from 1887 until his death. His house at Forest Avenue and Dempster Street was built of grout, a mixture of sand, slaked lime, and lake gravel that was poured in place. It was razed in 1938 and the estate subdivided and developed.

Burnham & Root designed the George Watson Smith house, 1462 Ridge Avenue. Completed in 1883, it has survived relatively unchanged and testifies to the grand scale of the houses built on the ridge. Photograph by Jenny Thompson.

Chapter 4

Twentieth-Century Evanston

By the end of the nineteenth century many of Evanston's early residents had died. John Evans, Orington Lunt, Alonzo Burroughs, Orvis French, and Miner Raymond died in 1897. Exhausted by her labors for temperance, suffrage, human freedom, and world peace, Frances Willard died in 1898; so did Osro A. Crain, John J. Foster, and George H. Foster. John Carney and Charles J. Gilbert died in 1900. American involvement in the Spanish-American War at the end of the century thrust the country onto the world stage, a stage made unstable by political realignments in Europe and Asia. The death of England's Queen Victoria in January 1901 cast a long shadow over the new century as did the assassination of President William McKinley in Buffalo, New York, later that year.[275]

Change was also in the air in Evanston. In 1900 the once quiet village, which had burgeoned to a population of 19,259, began to experience the problems of the city. For more than a third of the year the water was unhealthful and had to be boiled. The health department had to inspect the water and ice delivered to homes by both ice companies and dairies. Cows had to be tested for tuberculosis. There were ninety-one complaints about outhouse nuisances; open garbage wagons that dripped onto the streets brought other complaints. Despite the discovery of an antitoxin, diphtheria still accounted for four deaths; scarlet fever claimed one victim.[276]

By 1900 the Evanston police force numbered twenty, but the police chief requested two more patrolmen and three new bicycles "as they are of invaluable service in answering calls that require immediate attention." That year there were eighty arrests for disorderly conduct, forty-five assault-and-battery cases, fifty-five violations of the bicycle ordinance, and fifty-nine violations of the liquor ordinance.[277]

Temperance, the dream of many early Evanstonians, especially the Methodists, remained a lively issue and still found many adherents. In 1900 the National Woman's Christian Temperance Union moved its headquarters to Evanston and ten years later erected a new office building behind Frances Willard's beloved "Rest Cottage."[278] Anna Adams Gordon, who had been the close friend of Frances Willard, continued the battle against liquor and was elected president of the national group.[279]

Another of Frances Willard's causes had been woman's suffrage. She was joined by Catherine Waugh McCulloch who spent her legal talents and energies lobbying in Springfield from 1890 to 1913. After receiving a law degree from Union College of Law in Chicago, she was admitted to the Illinois Bar in 1886 and was one of the first woman lawyers in Chicago to achieve prominence in the profession. She was the first woman elected justice of the peace in Cook County, serving two terms in Evanston from 1907 to 1913, and she was the first woman to serve as Master of Chancery for the Superior Court of Cook County.[280] She conducted court in her home while her children played about. In every state she fought for the rights of women and children. "She knew how to lead and she knew how to follow. . . . She was unafraid of unpopular causes. . . . Her sense of humor eased the jolts of the journey, cleared the fog in many meetings."[281] Once the legislature gave women the right to vote for offices not expressly forbidden by the Constitution, her fellow Evanstonians gave her a rousing victory welcome in Fountain Square when she returned from Springfield in 1913.[282]

The national headquarters of the Woman's Christian Temperance Union was built in 1910 behind Frances Willard's "Rest Cottage." Designed by Charles R. Ayars, the carefully detailed red brick structure houses offices and archives for the large constituency of the national organization. Photograph by Jenny Thompson.

Anna Adams Gordon (1853-1931), at one time Frances Willard's private secretary, later served as president of the National Woman's Christian Temperance Union as well as of the world organization. Author of a well-known biography of Frances Willard, she also wrote a number of books for children. Photograph by Veeder, Albany, New York.

Catherine Waugh McCulloch (1862-1945), the noted lawyer and leader in the battle for woman's suffrage, served both as a justice of the peace and as a master in chancery, the first woman to hold this office in Cook County. Photograph by Moffett.

Care of the elderly emerged as another community goal. At a time when medical discoveries were prolonging life, smaller houses were altering the traditional living pattern in which several generations lived under one roof. The Swedish were the first to select Evanston as the place to build a retirement home. Many of the people had come to Evanston as pioneers and wanted to remain. In 1909, Swedish Societies Association commissioned the architect Andrew Sandegren to design its home for the elderly at 2320 Pioneer Avenue.[283]

The home of Catherine Waugh McCulloch and her husband Frank at 2236 Orrington Avenue was built in 1895. The Queen Anne house was designed by the architectural firm of Raeder Coffin & Crocker. Photograph by Henry E. Sorgerson.

The Swedish Retirement Home, 2320 Pioneer Road, was designed by the architect Andrew Sandegren (1869-1924). Completed in 1909, it was the first building of the complex that stretches between Grant and Colfax streets. Photograph courtesy of Evanston Photographic Studio.

In 1910, Evanston African-Americans numbered 1,160, or 4.96% of the 24,978 total population.[284] Leaders in the black community dedicated a Y.M.C.A. for African-Americans at 1014 Emerson Street.[285] Realtor William S. Mason and his wife Mary Mason donated land in front of Foster School to the District 75 School Board; Foster Field became a focal point for the African-American community, which lived largely on the west side.[286] In 1914 Dr. Isabella M. Garnett Butler, who had been the first African-American girl to graduate from Evanston Township High School, with her physician husband Arthur D. Butler founded the Evanston Sanitarium and Training School in their home at 1918 Asbury Avenue to provide a health center for Evanston's African-American residents. The Butlers moved into the small frame house behind the hospital to devote as much space as possible to their patients.[287]

Dr. Isabella Maude Garnett Butler (1872-1948), a graduate of the Provident Hospital Nurses' Training School, received her M. D. in 1901 from the Physicians' and Surgeons' College (now the Medical School of the University of Illinois). For her contributions to medical care a sixteen-acre park along the canal was named in her honor in 1975; it lies adjacent to the former location of the Community Hospital, which she helped establish in 1928 in the former home of Dr. Rudolph Penn at 2026 Brown Avenue. The Community Hospital closed in 1980.

As a place to live Evanston had always attracted writers: in 1900 the library staff counted 214 authors and composers living here.[288] Members of the Northwestern and Garrett faculties contributed many volumes. Especially popular were the novels written by Henry Kitchell Webster.[289] Lucy Fitch Perkins, who started her career as an illustrator of children's books and as a muralist, wrote *The Dutch Twins* in 1911, the first of her popular "Twin Series" that told about children of other lands and times.[290] Her friend, the poet and composer Louise Ayres Garnett, wrote *The Muffin Man, Master Will of Stratford*, and other books for young people.[291] Both women were active members of Alice C. D. Riley's Riley Circle, where they tried out their manuscripts and furthered their interest in the arts, both literary and visual.[292] In 1914 Jane Van Ettan Andrews composed the first opera written by an Illinois woman to be presented in America: *Guido Ferranti*, based on *The Duchess of Padua* by Oscar Wilde, was produced for the first time in Chicago by the Century Opera Company.[293]

With her husband, Dr. Arthur Daniel Butler, a graduate of Northwestern University, Dr. Isabella Butler established the fourteen-bed Evanston Sanitarium and Training School in 1914 in their home at 1918 Asbury Avenue (right) and they moved into the smaller house at 1916 Asbury Avenue (back, left). After her husband's death in 1924, she continued her efforts on behalf of the African American population's medical needs and helped found the Community Hospital. Photograph by Jenny Thompson.

Peter Christian Lutkin, dean of Northwestern's Music School, brought with him the dream of a great community music festival. With the construction of Patten Gymnasium on the university campus, there was an auditorium large enough to hold such a festival. Professor Arne Oldberg composed the "Festival Overture" that opened the first Chicago North Shore Music Festival in June 1909.[294] Over the years people thronged to hear world-famous performers like Ernestine Schumann-Heink, Alma Gluck, and Percy Grainger.[295] A chorus of 1,200 Evanston school children brought in a large segment of the community as performers. Public schools enriched their music programs and people began talking about Evanston's becoming the "musical center of the United States."[296]

Author, poet, and playwright Alice Cushing Donaldson Riley (1867-1955) was a dynamic force in Evanston's literary life. She fostered the written word in the Riley Circle, which met in her home, "The Lilacs," at 1822 Sheridan Road. Designed by Dwight Perkins, it was one of the four houses in the 1800 block demolished in 1980.

Lucy Fitch Perkins (1865-1937), a graduate of the Art School of the Boston Museum of Fine Arts, was on the first faculty of Pratt Institute, Brooklyn, New York. With a thriving career as a muralist and illustrator, she also turned to writing children's books. From The Goose Girl *(1906) to the twenty-five "Twins" books (1911 to 1936), she captured the hearts and minds of her young readers.*

The wealthy began to assemble collections of art. Realtor Charles Addison Wightman was known for his collection of fine paintings and rare books. He was associated with P. F. Volland in publishing the prints of Jules Guerin, the well-known artist whose beautiful renderings captured the soul of Daniel Burnham's 1909 *Plan of Chicago*.[297] Charles H. Chandler, who organized the artist's supply house of Thayer & Chandler and lived at 1733 Asbury Avenue, had a famous collection of Japanese prints.[298] Charles Frederick Grey, a pioneer entrepreneur in the hide and leather business in Chicago, moved to Evanston in spring 1866 and built a mansion at 1508 Forest Avenue where he hung the works of many distinguished painters; included were canvasses by Anton Mauve, Leon Perrault, Ferdinand Roybet, Adolphe William Bougereau, Thomas Moran, and William F. Richards. Grey gave several of these paintings to Evanston institutions and also donated land for the park at the northeast corner of Ridge Avenue and Main Street.[299]

The North Shore Music Festival, inaugurated in 1909, was held in the original Patten Gymnasium. This photograph of the interior shows the arched steel trusses that supported the roof and skylights. The festival breathed its last in 1939.

Theater received enthusiastic backing. Alice C. D. Riley and members of the Riley Circle organized the Drama Club in 1906 to foster community support.[300] The university and the high school presented stage productions. In 1911 C. G. Franklin built the Evanston Theater near Fountain Square for "polite vaudeville" and repertory groups that flourished with stars like Jessie Royce Landis and Guy Kibbie.[301] In the First Congregational Church, Marjorie Ayres Best founded the Pilgrim Players in fall 1918 and produced and directed religious dramas, which brought Evanston national recognition.[302] Motion pictures came to town with the opening in May 1913 of the Star Theater at 806 Davis Street.[303] Overprotective mothers probably frowned upon these dime movies as a rendezvous for their sons and daughters.

World War I began following the assassination on June 18, 1914, of the Austrian Archduke Francis Ferdinand and his wife Sophie in Sarajevo, the capital of the Austrian province of Bosnia. The suddenness of the hostilities caught a number of Evanstonians in Europe, including former mayor James A. Patten and his wife, Amanda, whom the Germans mistakenly arrested as spies in early August.[304] Aid to the overrun Belgians soon became a project of the Woman's Club, and Lucy Fitch Perkins wrote *The Belgian Twins* and *The French Twins* to promote relief for the war's first victims. The United States entered the war in April 1917 "to make the world safe for democracy." Two Evanstonians became generals—banker Charles Gates Dawes and George Van Horn Moseley, a graduate of the military academy at West Point.[305] John Henry Wigmore, the dean of the Northwestern Law School, was appointed to the office of the Judge Advocate General and helped draft the selective service legislation.[306] Walter Dill Scott, who had been the first professor of applied psychology at Carnegie Institute of Technology, drew up the world's first military personnel classification system.[307] A chemistry professor at Northwestern, Winford Lee Lewis, invented the deadly poison gas that bore his name—lewisite— which would have become a new military weapon had the war not come to an end.[308]

John Henry Wigmore (1863-1943), dean of the Northwestern Law School from 1901 to 1929, was also a well-known authority on Japan and author of the Treatise on the Anglo-American System of Evidence in Trials at Common Law *(commonly called "Wigmore on Evidence"). With his wife Emma Hunt Vogl Wigmore, he lived at 207 Lake Street from 1903 to 1934. Photograph by Eugene L. Ray.*

Oliver Baty Cunningham (1894-1918), son of a prominent civic leader, was killed just two months before the armistice was signed on November 11, 1918; his parents established in his remembrance the Cunningham Award, the highest honor for a male Evanston Township High School graduate.[309] Edward Hines, Jr., scion of the famous lumber family, was the first graduate of the Officers' Training Camp at Fort Sheridan to die in active service in France; his parents donated half a million dollars for a Catholic school to be built west of Lake Forest and $1.6 million for the construction of Hines Veterans Hospital.[310] In memory of Thomas H. Garnett, an African-American soldier killed in the Meuse-Argonne drive, the city council changed the name of Ayars Place to Garnett Place.[311]

Walter Dill Scott (1869-1955), a member of Northwestern's psychology department from 1901 to 1920, applied psychology to mass merchandising and advertising. He rose to the presidency of the university in 1920; in 1939 he stepped down to become president emeritus. Scott Hall was named in his honor.

In the fall of 1919 Elizabeth Odell, with the support of Helen Dawes and Nellie Fitch Kingsley established the Community Kitchen at 600 Davis Street to feed the sick; they also provided meals for the well-to-do on Thursdays, traditionally the "maid's night out."[312] Servants had been a way of life in Evanston. The wealthy employed sizable staffs, usually recruited among recent immigrants. Even the family of the school superintendent could afford three maids on an annual salary of $1,200. However, ratification in 1913 of the constitutional amendment authorizing the federal graduated income tax and the need for workers in the defense industries soon marked the end of an era. Evanston families living in large mansions had to change their living patterns.

Greek temples and Gothic castles found little favor in the twentieth century. A number of architects were groping to develop an American design idiom; they scorned the Gothic and Renaissance buildings that had masqueraded as banks, libraries, schools, office buildings, and houses all over the country. They were Midwesterners, many of them Chicago-reared. The dominant leader was a daring young man from Wisconsin who settled in Oak Park—Frank Lloyd Wright. Wright favored long, low, horizontal lines, rows of windows, open interior plans, and materials indigenous to the area. For a time Wright worked in Dwight Perkins' loft studio in Steinway Hall, alongside Myron Hunt and Robert C. Spencer, Jr. Perkins, Hunt, and Spencer had all attended the architecture school at the Massachusetts Institute of Technology; Wright, who had attended the University of Wisconsin, had worked for Louis Sullivan. Sullivan's mottos, "form follows function," served as an inspiration. Cross-fertilizing each other's designs, they became known as the architects of the Prairie School.[313]

Lawrence Bradford Perkins (1907-1997) and his father Dwight Heald Perkins (1867-1941) represent two generations of Chicago architecture. The elder Perkins worked for Burnham & Root before establishing his own office. Architect of the Chicago Board of Education from 1905 to 1911, he became well-known as an innovative designer of schools. His son was one of the founders of The Perkins & Will Partnership; the firm collaborated in 1939 with Eliel Saarinen on Winnetka's Crow Island School, one of the landmarks of modern architecture.
Courtesy Lawrence B. Perkins.

Dwight Perkins described what his architectural education was like during the late 1880s:

The Massachusetts Institute of Technology was the best school at the time . . . . The original thinkers had not appeared. At the institute we were taught to compose a plan and develop elevations to it as they would in any Italian Renaissance country. We were a branch of the School of Fine Arts in Paris. Our problems were real enough but they were not real in the sense of being built in America at the present day. . . . The principal instructor was Eugene J. Letang. He was a graduate of the School of Fine Arts, Paris. He was, according to the standards of the time, simply superb. He was a great reasoner and a wonderful designer and he had the proper composition which makes teachers out of men. . . . On the whole our work was only secondary to the library. There we got our clues and then—after two days of preliminary study we handed in our small sketches— and for the rest of the month we worked on the larger scale drawings, but always according to the limits imposed by our first sketch. That was the Institute for us. And according to the time, 1885 to 1887, it was O.K.—the best we could have gotten anywhere.[314]

Perkins added, "It was not until the close of the last century that I came under the influence of Louis Sullivan that I began to solve problems that were real—and I hope good looking also."[315] Sullivan, who had attended M.I.T. about a decade earlier, also spoke of the "unreal" character of what he had been taught to design there and later at the Ecole des Beaux Arts in Paris.[316]

Myron Hunt attended Northwestern University before transferring to M.I.T. He and his bride, Harriet, returned to Evanston in January 1895.[317] He designed a number of double houses, a popular form in the late nineteenth century, and a handsome shingled house for his own family at 1627 Wesley Avenue.[318] One of his most important early works is the red brick double house whose striking horizontality dominates the northeast corner of Ridge Avenue and Dempster Street; it was built in 1897 for the wealthy widow Catherine White.[319] He made another significant contribution to the city's residential stock when he designed several apartment buildings on the edge of the central business district—the Hereford, the Boylston, and the Cambridge—that solved a growing need in suburban communities. They had all the necessary conveniences, yet because they remained residential in scale, they did not disturb the single-family ambiance of a suburban town.

In 1905 Frank Lloyd Wright designed a house at 2420 Harrison Street, one of his early attempts to develop a house for people of modest means.[320] Compact, almost a cube in form, it lacks the cantilevers and horizontal lines typical of Wright's full-blown Prairie masterpieces. Legend has it that Wright himself considered it not very good, but good enough for Evanston. With its smug claim to be the "Athens of the Northwest," Evanston was not likely to find favor with the iconoclastic Wright. In 1917 newspaper headlines proclaimed that Wright was to design houses for a new development in northwest Evanston, but only one at 2614 Lincolnwood Drive was completed. Wright's name is on the building permit, but the design is quite simple in comparison with his other works of this period.[321] It is not acknowledged on any of the "official" lists of his work.

Myron Hunt, who studied at Northwestern and graduated from the Massachusetts Institute of Technology, built this house at 1627 Wesley Avenue for his wife Harriet Boardman Hunt. During his early association with Dwight Perkins, Robert C. Spencer, Jr., and Frank Lloyd Wright in Steinway Hall, Hunt's affinity for the ideas of the Prairie School deepened; in 1903 he moved to California and went into partnership with Elmer Grey. Photograph by Jenny Thompson.

The Hereford Apartments, 1637 Chicago Avenue, provided a transition in scale and massing between the growing central business district and the residential area to the north. Designed by Myron Hunt in 1899, the building was razed in 1978 despite a strong protest by the Evanston Preservation Commission.

Catherine White, widow of lawyer Hugh A. White, commissioned Myron Hunt to design the double house at 1307-13 Ridge Avenue in 1897. The horizontality and symmetry emphasized by the brick string course and flat-arched windows presage some of the Prairie School precepts that Frank Lloyd Wright would formulate after the turn of the century. Photograph by Jenny Thompson.

The stucco and wood house built for speculation for the Charles Browne Estate at 2420 Harrison Street is one of Frank Lloyd Wright's early solutions to the problem of designing aesthetically pleasing low-cost housing, an idea that would reappear later in his development of the Usonian house. Photograph by Jenny Thompson.

Dwight Perkins moved to Evanston and in 1904 built a home for his family at 2319 Lincoln Street.[322] He designed a number of houses in the Prairie style, but his chief claim to architectural fame rests on the forty schools he designed as staff architect of the Chicago Board of Education. Carl Schurz High School on Milwaukee Avenue is the best known.[323] A long-time conservationist, he also devoted twenty-five years of his life to the establishment and development of the Cook County Forest Preserve.[324]

In 1904 Dwight and Lucy Fitch Perkins moved into the house that he designed at 2319 Lincoln Street. The grounds were landscaped by noted landscape architect Jens Jensen. Both Perkins and Jensen were active in establishing the Cook County Forest Preserve system. For his contributions Evanston's only tract of forest preserve was named for Dwight Perkins.

The pair of houses at 1416 Church Street and 1631 Ashland Avenue that Walter Burley Griffin designed for banker Hurd Comstock, the grandson of Harvey B. Hurd, were built in 1911-12. Planned to share an enclosed garden and a double garage that was, however, never built, the two Comstock houses were built as rental units. The presentation drawings by Marion Mahony Griffin are in the art collection of Northwestern University. Photographs by Jenny Thompson.

Walter Burley Griffin, who worked for a while with the group in Steinway Hall and later in Wright's Oak Park studio, designed some of the most important Prairie School houses in Evanston: the two-flat at 1710 Asbury Avenue, built for Mary H. Bovee in 1908; 1024 Judson Avenue, built for Elsie Jenks and Frederick B. Carter, Jr., in 1910; and two houses for banker Hurd Comstock at 1416 Church Street and 1631 Ashland Avenue, planned to share a common garden and built for speculation in 1911-12. In 1912 Griffin won the international competition to design the plan of Canberra, the capital of Australia. He and his architect wife, Marion Mahony Griffin, (one of the first women to receive a B.S. in architecture at the Massachusetts Institute of Technology and the senior assistant designer in Wright's Oak Park studio), moved to Australia in 1914 and remained there the rest of their lives.[325] John S. Van Bergen, a younger and later associate of Frank Lloyd Wright, designed two houses in Evanston in 1915, one of brick at 1026 Michigan Avenue for the realtor George S. Ballard, and the other of stucco over concrete block at 741 Sheridan Road for Harold R. White. Two years later Van Bergen opened an office here, but soon closed it when he enlisted in the armed forces.[326]

The lakefront home of Harold R. White was one of John S. Van Bergen's experiments in the use of stucco over concrete block. Completed in 1915, the house at 741 Sheridan Road shows the influence of Frank Lloyd Wright and has elegantly patterned leaded glass.
Photograph by Jenny Thompson.

Another of the Prairie School architects who lived in Evanston was Thomas Eddy Tallmadge. Like many young architects he worked in the office of D. H. Burnham & Company, where he met his future partner, Vernon S. Watson. Tallmadge & Watson designed many houses in the Prairie idiom in Evanston and in Oak Park, where Watson lived. Among their first designs here is a house for the real estate firm of Quinlan & Tyson at 1112 Asbury Avenue.[327] After the waning of the Prairie style after World War I, Tallmadge & Watson turned to more traditional architectural forms for inspiration and designed houses and churches in revival styles in the Chicago area.[328]

Architect and historian Thomas Eddy Tallmadge, with his partner, Vernon Spencer Watson, played a leading role in the Prairie School. Architect of houses, churches, schools, and factories, Tallmadge is affectionately remembered by Evanstonians as the designer of the gracious ornamental streetlights installed throughout the city in 1931.

Although a few historians blamed the eclipse of the Prairie style by revivalism and eclecticism on the women who desired traditional houses that could be furnished with period furniture, Tallmadge himself, who was an historian as well as an architect, felt that "the failure of this style to rise beyond the generation may be ascribed to several factors: it never became fashionable. Not enough people of consequence adopted it to give it authority with the general herd."[329] However, this was not true in Evanston. Myron Hunt counted among his clients Harvey B. Hurd, the highly respected first president of the village board of trustees and a wealthy landowner. His daughter, Eda Hurd Lord, engaged Dwight Perkins and George W. Maher to design several houses when she developed the property that she inherited from her father and opened Elinor Place. Hurd's grandson, Hurd Comstock, hired Walter Burley Griffin. John Taylor Pirie, Jr., scion of the department store family, commissioned Hunt to design his house at 1330 Church Street. Another of Hunt's patrons was Catherine White, the wealthy widow of the lawyer Hugh A. White. A block south of her large double house on Ridge Avenue, Hunt also designed a house for Chancellor Livingston Jenks, Jr., the son of one of the principal developers of North Evanston. His cousin, Elsie Jenks Carter, had Griffin design her handsome house.

Designed by Tallmadge & Watson in 1906, the house at 1112 Asbury Avenue was built for $3,000 for Quinlan & Tyson. It was exhibited in the Chicago Architectural Club the same year and published in the Ladies' Home Journal in 1910. Photograph by Jenny Thompson.

Just north of his own house Myron Hunt designed the residence at 1330 Church Street for John Taylor Pirie, Jr. (1871-1940). Built in 1898 and exhibited at the Chicago Architectural Club and published in the Architectural Review in 1902, it continued to bring Hunt notoriety for the next several years. Photograph by Jenny Thompson.

Realtor Charles Addison Wightman was another patron of the Prairie School. He commissioned Robert C. Spencer, Jr. to design his first house at 1743 Wesley Avenue as well as three well-sited little cottages that he built for speculation on Pioneer Road just north of Lincoln Street, which were highly publicized from the time they were built in 1895.[330] Wightman had George W. Maher design the University Building at the northwest corner of Chicago Avenue and Davis Street where he had his real estate office.

Founder and first president of the Evanston Real Estate Board, Charles Addison Wightman (1861-1934) had Robert C. Spencer, Jr. design a group of three houses on Pioneer Road in 1895. The center one is known as "The Doll's House" because of an article on Elizabeth Gordon who used it as the model for one of her "Cranford" doll houses. Photograph by Jenny Thompson.

For the millionaire "Wheat King," James A. Patten, the well-known philanthropist who became mayor of Evanston from 1901 to 1903 and president of Northwestern's board of trustees from 1917 to 1920, Maher designed the beautiful granite mansion that once stood at 1426 Ridge Avenue, probably the most significant building ever built in Evanston. Maher also designed the gymnasium that Patten donated to Northwestern University, as well as Swift Hall of Engineering.[331] In 1908 Maher presented a plan for Northwestern's campus "that brilliantly recognized the aesthetic potential of the university's lakeside setting. But unfortunately the plan was not adopted, even in a modified form, and for another 60 years Northwestern turned its back on Lake Michigan, as though embarrassed by the natural beauty of the site."[332]

The "Wheat King" James A. Patten (1852-1928), nephew of John L. Beveridge, served as Evanston's mayor from 1901 to 1903 and as president of Northwestern's board of trustees from 1917 to 1920. His philanthropy extended to many local institutions, including Evanston Hospital, the Y.M.C.A., the Central Association of Evanston Charities, and many churches.

Amanda Louisa Buchanan Patten (1858-1935) devoted her life to charitable work and education. In addition to her duties as vice president of the Evanston Hospital board from 1906 until her death and as a member of the Evanston Township High School Board of Education, she also served as president of the University Guild, helped found the North Shore Music Festival, and established a twenty-acre goat farm to provide milk for hospitals. Photograph by J. D. Toloff.

The mansion at 1426 Ridge Avenue that George W. Maher designed for James and Amanda Patten was built in 1901 at a cost of approximately a half million dollars. Using the thistle as the "decorative motive" for the entire estate, Maher produced one of his most significant designs. Sold to a developer in 1938 for $50,000, the house and secondary buildings were demolished; all that remains are the fence, steps, and planters.

Northwestern's Patten Gymnasium was made possible by a $310,000 donation from the Pattens. The graceful curve of the façade expresses the great single-span arched vault under which was a baseball practice area that could be converted into a 4,500-seat auditorium. It was demolished in 1939.

Swift Hall of Engineering, also designed by George W. Maher, was completed in May 1909. A gift of $150,000 from Ann Higgins Swift (Mrs. Gustavus Franklin Swift) and her son Edward F. Swift enabled its construction. Using elegantly floriated decoration, Maher frames and divides the facade. During World War II, the building was renamed the Naval Science Building and was used to house the Navy College Training Program. The building, which today houses the psycholgy department, is once again called Swift Hall.

Tallmadge attributed another reason to the failure of the Prairie School to impress the fashion setters of the East:

> *It challenged, attacked and locked horns with the Beaux Arts, the great architectural school in Paris, when that school was at the height of its influence in America. This meant the hostility of all the East, particularly of New York, where most of the Paris men were working. It also meant the hostility of the architectural schools in America, where Beaux Arts methods of teaching universally prevailed.*[333]

Since the days when Greek Revival was popular with the settlers in Ridgeville, most laymen looked east to the land that they left behind. The influence of the 1893 World's Columbian Exposition lived on and people still greatly admired the works of the eastern architects—McKim Mead & White; Richard Morris Hunt; Peabody & Stearns; and George B. Post. The ideas of Louis Sullivan and Frank Lloyd Wright were not the "lost cause" that Tallmadge bemoaned, although it would take two world wars and a major economic depression to change that "lost cause" into a major triumph in later years.[334]

For those of more modest means, the clapboard-covered cottage, popular since the Civil War, was supplanted in the early twentieth century by the bungalow. The bungalow had a low, sloping roof, wide, overhanging eaves that emphasized the building's closeness to the ground, and picture windows that made the outdoors part of the indoor living experience. These were Prairie School features, but much scaled down and corrupted, to be sure. The name "bungalow" came from India and described the low, thatched houses of the Bengalese, but, as Lewis Mumford said, "the bungalows were the first designs that put California esthetically on the modern map."[335] As Evanstonians began to move west, especially to southern California, the city of Pasadena became a favorite and even had an Evanston Avenue. It seemed inevitable that the bungalow would reach Evanston; it was a cozy, inexpensive design, gobbling up little land per dwelling unit, while providing privacy and the greensward, albeit small, that many Americans desired.

Bungalows began to rise as quickly as weeds on vacant lots everywhere, especially in north and west Evanston where land was still available. In 1909 the *Evanston Index* described why bungalows were a popular form of house.[336] Henry Lawrence Wilson, "the bungalow man," successfully promoted them in *The Bungalow Book*:

> *In the Bungalow, if properly designed, is combined grace, beauty and comfort at a minimum cost. . . . the problem of easy housekeeping and homemaking is reduced almost to an exact science. . . . Entrance is usually into a large living room—the room where the family gathers, and in which the visitor feels at once the warm, homelike hospitality. Everything in this room should suggest comfort and restfulness.[337]*

Also popular was the book by Frederick T. Hodgson, *Practical Bungalows and Cottages for Town and Country*; many people agreed with Hodgson's assessment, "There is nothing either affected or insincere about these little houses. They are neither consciously artistic nor consciously rustic. They are the simple and unconscious expression of the needs of their owners, and as such they can be credited with the best kind of architectural propriety."[338]

Although many bungalows are similar, closer study reveals their individuality. Ideal for small lots, most were only one story, but had dormers in the low-pitched roofs that made the attic usable.

Shingled or stuccoed or made of brick, most bungalows have simple, geometric ornamentation on the porch piers. Some people enclosed the porch as part of their living area, thus creating a sunroom. Interiors often had exposed beams, painted plaster walls, and curved archways between the rooms. In 1920 R. B. Williamson designed an interesting collection of bungalows on Thayer Street that impart a real California feeling in the wide eaves and use of wood.[339]

Industrialists and business leaders continued to move to Evanston for the same reasons as they had in the late nineteenth century. Some brought their industries and businesses with them. In 1901 A. J. Rollert requested permission to build an addition to a structure on Custer Avenue that would be used for offices and storage for his Original Manufacturing Company.[340] Trying to grapple with the issue of industry within the city limits, the city council passed an ordinance that stipulated "that any building or portion thereof where any manufacturing of merchandise with machinery operated by steam, gas, electricity or other mechanical power, or in which the operations of any merchandise business carried on or conducted therein, steam, gas, electricity, or other mechanical power is used, shall be deemed a factory." No such building could be erected or altered without an application accompanied by complete plans. The ordinance required fire escapes and prohibited a factory from operating on Sunday, although there were no penalties for violations.[341] While the aldermen debated, Rollert kept on building and began mandamus proceedings against the city to force the issuance of a permit. The situation became more confused each day. The city council passed a resolution to have Rollert arrested, but Mayor James A. Patten refused to carry out the order and challenged the aldermen to impeach him if they desired. During the weeks of controversy and discussion, Rollert succeeded in establishing the first industry within the city's borders.[342]

In 1900 Clayton Mark opened a factory to manufacture well supplies at Dempster Street and Dodge Avenue, at that time outside the city limit.[343] Mark Manufacturing Company offered job opportunities to a large group of people who emigrated from northwest Poland and settled in modest wooden cottages near the factory. Father Felix Feldheim, the popular pastor of Ascension of Our Lord Church, worked hard to promote the annexation of the neighborhood south of Crain Street and west of Florence Avenue, where early settlers had long ago cleared the land to grow vegetables for the Chicago market. Its annexation in 1913 served to control the liquor industry and the "blind pigs" that had sprung up on the edge of the area, much to the consternation of residents and civic leaders.[344]

After the factories came the apartments, although few of the factory workers could afford to live in them. The first apartment buildings had been built close to the business district as early as the 1880s; by the second decade of the twentieth century they had become a way of life. Some, like the Boylston, Cambridge, and Hereford apartments by Myron Hunt, blended with Evanston's suburban atmosphere, but as Rogers Park began to fill with apartment buildings, Evanstonians reconsidered the issue. In 1913 residents of the Germania Subdivision south of Calvary Cemetery petitioned the city to disannex because they felt that they were not receiving their share of city services. Evanstonians, fearing that the area would become totally filled with apartments, voted the following year for its disannexation and it became part of Chicago.[345]

The North Shore Hotel replaced the Avenue House on the northeast corner of Chicago Avenue and Davis Street. Designed by Robert S. DeGolyer, the $1.5 million six-story Tudor building opened amid great fanfare in 1919. Today the building houses an assisted living retirement community and is known as the North Shore Retirement Hotel.

Victor C. Carlson's first venture in the Evanston central business district was the Library Plaza Hotel, built in 1922. After acquiring and demolishing Fowler's Photographic Studio and the building that housed the Cellini Shop, Carlson built an annex to the Library Plaza Hotel, the Carlson Building. Completed in 1928, the nine-story structure at 636 Church Street provided office space for the medical professions.

The Georgian Hotel, built in 1926, on Davis Street and Hinman Avenue, was demolished to make way for a new structure to house a Mather Lifeways retirement facility.

The Homestead Hotel at 1625 Hinman Avenue was built in 1928. It was listed on the National Register of Historic Places in February 2006. Photograph by Jenny Thompson.

The Ridgeview Hotel (built 1924) was converted into a long-term care facility in 1971. Photograph by Jenny Thompson.

The Evanshire Hotel (1923) at Hinman Avenue and Main Street.
The Georgian, Homestead, Ridgeview, and Evanshire hotels brought the convenience of apartment life to many
Evanstonians. Located on the edges of the business districts, they offered convenience and elegance to those who no longer
wished to maintain single-family residences. Photograph by Jenny Thompson.

Before the outbreak of the war in 1914 Evanston's building department issued permits for apartments with as many as thirty units. However, as neighborhood hostility grew, people began agreeing not to sell their property for apartment sites. In 1915 the city council set a limit on flat buildings.[346] In 1916, after more than 175 units had been built, the city established "restricted residential district" and adopted a building code requiring a setback of seventeen feet from the street.[347] The city also passed a new smoke ordinance to control the density of emissions from apartment furnaces that burned soft coal.[348] Despite these restrictions, 76 more were constructed at a total cost of $1,259,800.[349] Plans were soon announced for a $2 million residential hotel—the North Shore—to replace the landmark Avenue House.[350] Apartments rented quickly, forcing a rise in land values, which in turn began to dictate smaller units. The one-room flat became the newest type of residential unit: the Claridge Apartments, designed by Walter Ahlschlager, rose at 319 Dempster Street and was described as "a bachelor's paradise."[351]

Building activity declined as the country devoted its energy and money to the war effort, although to encourage development the realtors Mason & Smart began to distribute pamphlets on how desirable Evanston was.[352] A. T. McIntosh & Company developed Centralwood, a five-block area on either side of Central Street, just west of the city limits; their advertisements offered land at only $9 a front foot. On April 18, 1916, Evanstonians voted 2,630 to 438 for its annexation. Long a haven for toughs and hoboes, as well as "blind pigs," the area came under police protection as a result.[353] Near the war's end in 1918, Evanston realtors organized the Evanston Real Estate Board, and elected as their first president Charles A. Wightman.[354]

With the passage in 1919 of the state statute permitting cities and towns to regulate land usage, a new tool became available. Evanston became the first city to make use of that law, passing the Municipal Zoning Ordinance of 1921. Evanston realtors approved the idea with enthusiasm; Quinlan & Tyson advertised that the ordinance would have "far reaching effects upon the future of Evanston along the line of stabilizing and increasing real estate values."[355] The ordinance set aside some areas for apartment buildings and others for commercial and industrial uses. Rules regulated the size of lots, the height of buildings, and their placement on the lot.[356] The zoning ordnance anticipated a population of 400,000, even though the city had grown only to 37,234 in 1920.

By the end of 1921, the *Evanston News-Index* once again reported a building boom and there was rapid expansion in the central business district. More construction was under way than there had been for years, "in spite of calamity howlers and idle workers."[357] Land values in the business and commercial areas inflated 500% and property on Fountain Square was selling for $2,500 a front foot.[358] Victor C. Carlson entered the development field and in 1922 erected Evanston's first seven-story building at 1633-41 Orrington Avenue—the Library Plaza Hotel.[359] A block north he had the Orrington Hotel built in 1923-24.[360] On the site of Northwestern's first building, he had the John Evans Apartments erected in 1925, designed by the architect Stanley M. Peterson.[361] In 1928 Carlson built the nine-story Carlson Building at 636 Church Street, adjacent to the Library Plaza Hotel; it provided office space for doctors and dentists.[362] The Georgian Hotel, developed by Henry Paschen and Albert Pick and their architect Albert S. Hecht at 422 Davis Street, joined other residential hotels near the downtown area when it was formally opened in January 1927.[363] Architect Philip A. Danielson and his wife Ruby opened the 200-room Homestead Hotel at 1625 Hinman Avenue the following year.[364] The same thing was happening in the south end of town along Main Street. At the southwest corner of Main Street and Forest Avenue, Louis N. Nelson and Frank C. Lewin built the Evanston Hotel, which opened in 1916.[365] The Ridgeview Hotel at 901-909 Maple Avenue was built in 1924 for those desiring the convenience of residential hotel living.[366] The 128-room Evanshire Hotel, designed by the architect John A. Nyden, opened in 1923 at the southwest corner of Hinman Avenue and Main Street.[367]

In 1926 Henry C. Lytton & Sons became the first State Street store to open a branch in downtown Evanston.[368] In March 1929 Marshall Field & Company announced its move to Evanston, and the new store opened in November.[369] However, with the stock market crash and the onset of the depression in 1929, further expansion ceased and plans had to be filed away until the economic crisis had eased. By the mid-1930s there began to be some signs of recovery and a revitalized economy. In 1936 John M. Smyth & Company established a branch of its Chicago furniture store on Church Street; four years later they built a new four-story showroom.[370] In August 1945 the clothing firm of Maurice L. Rothschild announced plans to erect a $500,000 store on the site of the Rood Building, which they planned to raze. After a fire gutted the Rood Building on February 15, 1946, they demolished it and proceeded with their plans; the new store opened in March 1948.[371] Fountain Square and downtown Evanston soon had the highest concentration of quality stores in the Chicago Area outside the Loop.

Evanstonians gathered in 1929 for the laying of the cornerstone of Marshall Field & Company on the northwest corner of Sherman Avenue and Church Street, once the site of Haven School. With elegant Art Deco ornamentation and a corner clock reminiscent of the flagship State Street store, the finished building provided a handsome anchor for Evanston's downtown.

In 1940 John M. Smyth & Company made a commitment to Evanston by building a new structure at 820-24 Church Street next to the store they had been occupying for four successful years. Although John M. Smyth left Evanston in 1976, the building held a succession of financial institutions, a bookshop and the offices of Scandinavian Design. It now houses a branch of First Bank and Trust. Built of Bedford stone trimmed in red granite, it was described as "modified traditional in design." Photograph by Jenny Thompson.

Designed by John T. Wilson Jennings, the Rood Building occupied the south end of the triangle between Orrington and Sherman avenues since 1895. The destructive fire that reduced it to ruins in 1946 precipitated changes to Fountain Square. Photograph courtesy of Evanston Photographic Studio.

Fountain Square itself was dramatically transformed. Since its dedication on July 4, 1876, the three-tiered cast iron Centennial Fountain had been the heart of downtown Evanston. However, in 1946 the fountain was removed to relieve traffic congestion, and on Armistice Day 1949 War Memorial Fountain, designed by architect Hubert Burnham, was dedicated as the focal point of the relocated Fountain Square in front of the Rothschild Building.[372] Centennial Fountain was moved to Merrick Rose Garden and rededicated July 4, 1951.[373] In 1976 the War Memorial Fountain was superseded by the Bicentennial Fountain, a three-fountain complex with three brick piers with bronze plaques inscribed with the names of Evanstonians who had sacrificed their lives in the nation's wars.[374] Once the city had moved its offices into the former Evanston Country Club at the northeast corner of Oak Avenue and Lake Street, the old City Hall designed by Holabird & Roche was razed. Its site was acquired by Walter P. Powers who put up a four-story commercial building whose principal tenant was Three Sisters.[375] On the southwest corner of Fountain Square the First National Bank erected a five-story building in the colonial style; designed by Naess & Murphy, it was completed in 1955.[376]

A comparison of Fountain Square before 1946 and after 1949 shows City Hall replaced by the commercial block that housed Three Sisters; the Rood Building, by Maurice L. Rothschild; and the 1876 Centennial Fountain, by the 1949 War Memorial Fountain. Photographs courtesy of Evanston Photographic Studio.

Evanston, with its proximity to Chicago, good transportation, and reputation as a "city of homes," began to attract a number of large companies. Washington National Life Insurance Company moved its headquarters to Evanston in 1936 and became one of the city's largest employers.[377] Sentinel Radio Corporation moved to Evanston in 1939; when its new offices at 2100 Dempster Street were completed in 1946, Foster G. McGaw moved his American Hospital Supply into 2020 Ridge Avenue, Sentinel's former location.[378] In 1939 Rust-Oleum Corporation, which manufactured the rust-preventative coating developed by Captain Robert Fergusson, purchased land in Evanston and built a plant at 2425 Oakton Street that soon covered twelve acres.[379] Pelouze Scale and Manufacturing Company, founded in 1894, moved into the building at 1218 Chicago Avenue in September 1946.[380] Two years later Hibbard, Spencer & Bartlett built the largest hardware warehouse in the world on Howard Street at Hartrey Avenue. In a building covering seventeen acres, the company employed a work force of 650 people.[381] From 1949 to 1951 Earl Muntz manufactured a racing car—the Muntz Jet—at 1000 Grey Avenue. He later converted the building into a television assembly plant that employed 250 people.[382] Shure Brothers, manufacturers of microphones and electronic components, built an 80,000-square-foot-plant at 222 Hartrey Avenue in 1954-55.[383] By 1968 Evanston had over seventy industrial firms to support its tax base.[384]

The southwest corner of Fountain Square, occupied since 1900 by the City National Bank, saw the erection in 1955 of a new building for its successor, First National Bank, designed by Naess & Murphy.

An article in the *Chicago Tribune* on Sunday, May 7, 1961, pointed out that twenty-eight organizations, associations, and foundations had established their national or international headquarters in Evanston. Based upon a proposal of the Plan Commission in 1966, the city embarked upon a concerted effort to attract large offices, businesses, and organizations: Evanston gained the reputation and the sobriquet of "Headquarters City."[385] By 1976 fifty-four groups had located their headquarters here; among them were Rotary International, Packaging Corporation of America, National Merit Scholarship Corporation, American Academy of Pediatrics, United Methodist Church, Association of American Medical Colleges, National Foundation of Funeral Service, Soiltest, Textile Bag Manufacturers Association, and General Finance Corporation.[386]

While the city was busy with its economic development, the university continued to grow and found it necessary to provide additional housing and expand its educational facilities. Eleven men's dormitories arranged in quadrangles were built north of Patten Gymnasium. Designed by the New York architectural firm, Palmer, Hornbostel & Jones, they were ready in February 1914. A new structure to house the social sciences, Harris Hall, went up south of University Hall. Named for its major benefactor,

Norman Wait Harris and dedicated December 1915, it was designed by the famous Boston firm Shepley, Rutan & Coolidge.[387]

Harris Hall (1915) was the first building built in the twentieth century on the south end of the Northwestern campus. The three-story limestone structure, designed by Shepley Rutan & Coolidge, contains classrooms, offices, a social hall, and a 300-seat auditorium.

In order to consolidate its professional schools, during the 1920s Northwestern acquired land for a second campus in Chicago. The trustees called upon James Gamble Rogers to draw up the master plan in 1922. After Rogers, who started his architectural practice in Chicago, moved to New York, he gained national recognition for his design in 1917 of Harkness Memorial Tower and Quadrangle at Yale University.[388] Throughout the 1920s and 1930s Rogers catered to Northwestern's expansion, both in Chicago and Evanston. He was responsible for Dyche Stadium, which was completed in fall 1926; Deering Library, completed in December 1932; the Women's Quadrangle, built over the course of eleven years and completed in 1938; Scott Hall/Cahn Auditorium, which was finished in September 1941; and Lutkin Hall, built in 1941 to provide an auditorium for the School of Music.[389]

In 1939 the Walter P. Murphy Foundation donated over $6 million to establish the Technological Institute. The site proposed was that of Patten Gymnasium and Dearborn Observatory. Patten Gymnasium was summarily demolished, but the observatory was spared by moving it closer to the lake shore. Holabird & Root received the commission for the Technological Institute as well as that for the replacement gymnasium that was built north of the Men's Quadrangles. Dedicated June 1942, "Tech" housed not only the Engineering School but also the departments of chemistry and physics.[390]

To house the influx of veterans who enrolled after the end of World War II, the university erected villages of steel-craft and Quonset huts. More permanent housing was provided for faculty and staff when the Northwestern Apartments were built in1947 across from the Orrington Hotel.[391] The former Norwegian-Danish Theological Seminary at 1830 Sherman Avenue was purchased in 1950 for a men's dormintory.[392] Over the next decade Holabird, Root & Burgee designed several residence halls— Sargent, Shepard, Bobb, Elder, and Allison—to ease the housing shortage. They were also responsible for the new classroom building and the field house that had been major objectives of the centennial fund drive: Kresge Centennial Hall, completed in 1955, was named in honor of the Kresge Foundation, which had donated a total of $1.5 million, and McGaw Memorial Hall, completed in 1952, was named in honor of the Reverend Francis Alexander McGaw, the father of Foster G. McGaw.[393]

On October 14, 1960, Northwestern announced plans to expand the campus eastward with a seventy-four acre lakefill addition because "the acquisition of land to the west of the campus would impair the university's relation with Evanston because it would take valuable real estate off the tax rolls [and] crowding the existing campus with new buildings would destroy its open and spacious character."

It took almost a year to gain the approval of the city, county, and state, as well as the U.S. Army Corps of Engineers, and controversy about the source of the fill pursued the project until its dedication on October 7, 1964. One of Northwestern's most striking buildings went up on the northeast edge of the lakefill: the twin-towered Lindheimer Astronomical Research Center, designed by Skidmore, Ownings & Merrill, was completed in 1966. Skidmore, Owings & Merrill also received commissions for several other major structures on the lakefill: the new library, completed in 1969; the O. T. Hogan Biological Sciences Building, completed in 1970; and the Frances Searle Building, completed in 1973. All three were designed by Walter Netsch, Jr., who was also responsible for the Rebecca Crown Administrative Center, built 1965-68 on Clark Street over vacated Orrington Avenue.[394] Among the other large architectural commissions during the early 1970s, several went to the firm of Loebl, Schlossman, Bennett & Dart: on the original campus, Arthur Andersen Hall, Nathaniel Leverone Hall, and the Owen L. Coon Forum, and on the lakefill, Norris University Center and Pick-Staiger Concert Hall.[395]

Named for William A. Dyche, Northwestern's business manager, Dyche Stadium was completed in time for the 1926-27 school term. McGaw Memorial Hall, at the north end of the stadium, was built in 1952 for indoor spectator events. The stadium underwent extensive rennovations and improvements in 1995 and was renamed Ryan Stadium in 1997.

Deering Library occupied the center of the arc of buildings that once swept from Orrington Lunt Library to Harris Hall. Inspired by King's College Chapel, Cambridge, England, which was completed in 1515, James Gamble Rogers produced a "modified Gothic" structure that opened in December 1932.

Stretching the full block between Emerson Street and University Place on Sheridan Road, Scott Hall was completed in 1941. Named for former Northwestern president, Walter Dill Scott, it provided lounges, meeting rooms, and a cafeteria; the 1,225-seat Cahn Auditorium was named for Bertram Cahn for his munificent gift.

The enormous complex of the Technological Institute occupies the former sites of the original Patten Gymnasium and Dearborn Observatory. Its somber Lannon stone bulk is relieved only by stone carvings by the sculptor Edgar Miller. The complex underwent renovation in 1999, and today houses the Robert R. McCormick School of Engineering and Applied Science, and the departments of chemistry, physics, and astronomy.

However, the greatest visual change came to Evanston with the introduction of the skyscraper. In November 1969 State National Bank, successor to Thomas C. Hoag's first banking institution, moved into its third building on the same site at the northeast corner of Fountain Square. Its twenty-one story steel-and-glass tower dwarfed the rest of the city and set a new precedent.[396] It was followed in 1974 by the fourteen-story Holiday Inn at the northeast corner of Sherman Avenue and Lake Street. Once the city passed an ordinance in January 1972 that legalized the sale of liquor, its construction was assured.[397] In 1977 American Hospital Supply moved into the new eighteen-story office building at the northwest corner of Sherman Avenue and Grove Street.[398] The "grand old lady of the North Shore" would never be the same.

By 1980 Evanston's central business district had been dramatically altered: the new buildings of State National Bank and American Hospital Supply caused a drastic change in scale. Although the city lost a number of major retailers over the years, the downtown has continued to thrive. To house the influx of office workers and shoppers, the City of Evanston had to build a large parking structure on Sherman Avenue.

The domestic scene underwent a series of changes too. The restoration of Colonial Williamsburg, which was begun in 1927, inspired homeowners and architects to draw upon the architecture of the American colonies anew. In 1931, along the abandoned right-of-way of the old Glenview trolley line, Lawrence B. Perkins designed the first Cape Cod house in Evanston at 3003 Harrison Street.[399] In 1937 H. Ring Clauson designed a house in the colonial mode at 2501 Marcy Avenue, just west of the house by Perkins.[400] These colonial revival designs competed with innovative houses of the future at the Century of Progress Exposition, which was held in Chicago in 1933 and 1934 during the depths of the depression. George Fred Keck brought the sophisticated technology of steel and glass to residential design in the House of Tomorrow and the Crystal House. Howard T. Fisher developed and exhibited a house of load-bearing steel panels and glass; it had standardized parts that could be mass-produced. However, it would be left to the manufacturers of mobile homes eventually to capitalize on the idea of mass-produced residences.[401]

Having recently graduated from the College of Architecture of Cornell University, Lawrence B. Perkins designed a house for speculation at 3003 Harrison Street. In 1935 he would go into partnership with his college roommate, Philip Will, Jr., the start of one of the major architectural firms in the country. Photograph by Jenny Thompson.

The severely rectilinear house that Bertrand Goldberg (1913-1997) designed for Doris L. Mullen and Thomas H. Mullen is a surprising contrast to his later fascination with curved and rounded shapes manifested in such works as Marina City, the Raymond M. Hillard Center, and Prentice Women's Hospital. The Mullen house was moved in 1951 to 3200 Harrison Street. Photograph by Jenny Thompson.

The house that Philip Will, Jr. designed for his family at 2949 Harrison Street is still considered "modern" although it has been almost fifty years since it was built in 1937. Bands of casement windows relegated to the corners and horizontal board-and-batten siding produce a tightly organized design, one that relates the building closely to its narrow corner site.
Photograph by Jenny Thompson.

William Ferguson DeKnatel (1907-1973), a graduate of the Ecole des Beaux Arts and one of the first group of Taliesin Fellows to study under Frank Lloyd Wright, designed the house at 200 Dempster Street for Ellen Newby and Lambert H. Ennis, professor of English at Northwestern. Photograph by Jenny Thompson.

While steel as a building material for homes had little mass appeal, three wooden houses built in Evanston were prophetic. In 1936 Bertrand Goldberg designed an unadorned cube-like house at 2501 Central Park Avenue for the Thomas H. Mullen family; the little five-room cottage upset the conservative neighborhood, ever fearful of a decline in property values.[402] When Northminster Presbyterian Church built its new south facade in 1951, the house was moved further west to 3200 Harrison Street.[403] In 1937 Philip Will, Jr., who later became president of the American Institute of Architects, designed another controversial house at 2949 Harrison Street for his own family; he jokingly referred to it as the "Great Lakes oreboat style of architecture." With its horizontal board-and batten cypress siding and tailored, crisp lines, it recalls the Prairie houses of twenty-five years earlier.[404] In 1941, on a lot once part of Daniel Burnham's lakefront estate, William F. DeKnatel designed a house for Lambert H. Ennis. Its horizontal lines and bands of windows that overlook a woody, natural world also hark back to Prairie School precepts.[405]

Variations on the box occupied contemporary architects who designed houses in Evanston:

Architect David N. Haid's severely rectilinear steel, brick, and glass home, 1221 Michigan Avenue. Photograph by Jenny Thompson.

Kenneth A. Schroeder, Richard Whitaker, and Lloyd Gadau's design for the Charles H. Wilson house, 529 Judson Avenue, whose diagonal boards thrust beyond the cube. Photograph by Jenny Thompson.

The sober vertically sheathed home of architect Neil D. Anderson, 710 Sheridan Road. Photograph by Jenny Thompson.

As American troops were landing on the Normandy beaches in June 1944, Evanston was already looking for ways to solve the critical need for housing when the servicemen returned. Mayor Samuel Gilbert "Bert" Ingraham appointed the developer Clarence A. Hemphill as Chairman of the Citizens Advisory Committee on Postwar Planning.[406] A sub-committee studied the housing situation in Evanston and presented its interim report to the city council. The report cited Evanston's main housing problems: (1) mansions too expensive to maintain because of increased federal income taxes and the dearth of servants; (2) houses in need of rehabilitation, especially along the Chicago North Western Railroad tracks from Noyes Street to South Boulevard; (3) the need for better housing for low-income families; (4) the need for affordable housing for young couples; and (5) the need to protect existing real estate values.[407]

Big mansions were considered at the time obsolete white elephants. Because the zoning law forbade their conversion into apartments and because of the widely held notion that increased density would turn them into slums, demolition seemed the expedient answer; developers eager for their demise were ready to subdivide the estates and build smaller houses. Streets and sewers had already been installed in southwest Evanston before the depression years. In the rest of town there were occasional double lots that could be subdivided. For affordable housing the one-story ranch house began to take the place of the bungalow, while bi-level and tri-level houses offered innovative plans for houses that had to fit on smaller lots. To accommodate the children resulting from the rising birthrate, the school boards had to build five elementary schools and add new facilities to the high school to upgrade the educational program. The city made arrangements with the Metropolitan Sanitary District to use the banks of the Sanitary Canal for temporary housing, recreation, and institutional purposes.[408]

For those who desired custom-designed houses, a new generation of architects stood ready to refute the English cottages, Norman farmhouses, miniature Monticellos, and eclectic ranch houses that the developers built all over town. Some had studied at Armour Institute of Technology (now the Illinois Institute of Technology), inspired by the design concepts of its director Ludwig Mies van der Rohe, who fled to Chicago in 1938 from the political situation in Germany. His use of glass and steel and his doctrine of "less is more" would revolutionize building design. Frank Lloyd Wright continued as an important, if flamboyant, figure on the American scene. Some architectural students flocked to Wright's studios at Spring Green, Wisconsin, and Taliesin, Arizona; others wanted to study with Eliel Saarinen at the Cranbrook School in Bloomfield Hills, Michigan. Other European émigrés, Walter Gropius and Marcel Breuer, intrigued and inspired by the designs of Louis Sullivan and Frank Lloyd Wright when they appeared in Europe, began teaching at Harvard.

Architects continued to find Evanston a congenial city in which to settle. David N. Haid built a carefully detailed brick, glass, and steel Miesian home in 1968 for his family at 1221 Michigan Avenue.[409] The ad hoc partnership of Kenneth A. Schroeder, Richard Whitaker, and Lloyd Gadau designed a house of glass and wood for sculptor Charles H. Wilson at 529 Judson Avenue in 1973.[410] In 1974 Neil D. Anderson built a house for his family at 710 Sheridan Road.[411] Four years later George A. Larson moved into a contemporary frame house on the tree-shaded 1000-block of Michigan Avenue.[412] Inserted between Italianate villas and Queen Anne mansions, sometimes houses like these arouse neighborhood dismay, just as over the course of history each new architectural style probably provoked a similar response. However, with the patina of time they will be recognized as a new chapter of architectural history that ultimately contributes to Evanston's rich texture and variety. This pageant of changing architectural form reveals the values of successive generations of Evanstonians. In no other way do people set forth more clearly their cultural aspirations, their economic status, or their history: all civilizations have been judged by their buildings, and buildings have become their most convincing documents.

Evanston's changes are also recorded in the succession of its structures: from a time of plain living and high thinking to one of rich ostentation, from seeking reassurance in tradition to finding form in contemporary living and materials. Yet despite this diversity, order, not chaos, has been the result because the land itself always has the last word. The great elms planted by the settlers and the sweeping lawns unify the broad spectrum of domestic architecture built in Evanston since its earliest days.

Appendix A

Selected List of Architects and Their Works

Evanston's reputation as "the city of homes" developed over the years as block after block of its tree-shaded streets became ornamented with suburban villas designed by prominent local builders and well-known architects. When agents of Northwestern University platted the town in 1854, they imposed a grid pattern over the historical path of the Green Bay Trail, the ridge along which the pioneers had been living for almost twenty years. As developers laid out new subdivisions they accepted the grid as the standard to be followed. In 1874 Everett Chamberlin remarked, "Evanston differs from many suburbs—notably lakeshore suburbs—in respect to the manner in which it is laid out. Its streets run at right angles, and show no suspicion of a curve to the right or left. . . . the curved lines which form the distinguishing traits of some suburbs met with no approval. Evanston bears the stamp of its devoutly-inclined founders." Thus, long vistas are punctuated by a pleasing variety of architectural styles that reflect Evanston's building history.

To include every architect who worked in Evanston would have been impossible; hence, by necessity this appendix is a selected list. To keep it manageable but useful I have verified and augmented the preliminary list of houses drawn up by Margery B. Perkins. Each entry includes brief biographical data; other important structures by an architect or architectural firm; and a list of Evanston houses still extant as of September 1983, the owner for whom it was built, and the date of the original structure. Thus, neither additions nor remodelings have been taken into account. Inclusion does not necessarily imply particular merit on the part of the architect or the house, nor does it refer to the state of a structure's integrity: the list contains house that are noteworthy—on the National Register of Historic Places, significant structures in the Evanston Lakeshore Historic District or the Evanston Ridge Historic District, and/or Evanston Landmarks—as well as those that might escape the attention of an architectural historian. While the book traces the development of Evanston as a rich, vibrant community of people and dwellings, the appendix shows the chronological development of some of the architects and builders who helped create "the city of homes."

Barbara J. Buchbinder-Green, 1984

CHARLES ROBERT AYARS (1861-1934)
Charles R. Ayars spent his boyhood in Evanston and began his architectural practice here in the 1890s. For the most part, he designed residences for private clients as well as for contractors developing various areas of Evanston. He also designed small commercial buildings, Annie May Swift Hall on the Northwestern campus, and the WCTU Headquarters Building behind Frances Willard's "Rest Cottage."

1719 Asbury Avenue, Eliza J. Hinsdale, 1894
1425 Davis Street, William S. Young, 1896
1922 Orrington Avenue, Augie C. Griffin, 1896
1145 Asbury Avenue, Edward B. Griswold, 1897
936 Sheridan Road, Jonathan T. Currier, 1898
1215 Judson Avenue, Thaddeus W. Heermans, 1898

1217 Judson Avenue, Thaddeus W. Heermans, 1898
1221 Judson Avenue, Thaddeus W. Heermans, 1898
1140 Hinman Avenue, Arthur M. Shellito, 1898
1809 Asbury Avenue, George R. Work, 1898
1420 Davis Street, Jeannie Lord Ayars, 1899
1220 Judson Avenue, Frank R. Bissell, 1899
1243 Maple Avenue, Arthur W. Cooper, 1899
2127 Orrington Avenue, James Alden James, 1903
1117 Asbury Avenue, Allen A. Keene, 1903
2419 Lincoln Street, Charles R. Ayars, 1904
2040 Sheridan Road, Daniel Bonbright, 1905
1311 Wesley Avenue, Comstock Estate, 1906
1327 Dempster Street, Comstock Estate, 1906
2715 Harrison Street, Otto L. Braunhold, 1906
828 Colfax Street, Thomas B. Carson, 1908
900 Colfax Street, Thomas B. Carson, 1908
904 Colfax Street, Thomas B. Carson, 1908
2415 Harrison Street, A. V. Coffman, 1908
1220 Crain Street, John Schwender, 1908
818 Colfax Street, Thomas B. Carson, 1908
810 Colfax Street, Thomas B. Carson, 1908
917 Elmwood Avenue, Joel A. Holmgren, 1909
921 Elmwood Avenue, Joel A. Holmgren, 1909
925 Elmwood Avenue, Joel A. Holmgren, 1909
929 Elmwood Avenue, Joel A. Holmgren, 1909
631 Milburn Street, Betsy A. Bridge, 1909
925 Maple Avenue, Axel F. Carlson, 1909-10
2501 Harrison Street, Theo W. Chaffee, 1910
1619 Ashland Avenue, Henry S. Shedd, 1910
2525 Lincoln Street, Robert E. James, 1910
916 Elmwood Avenue, Joel A. Holmgren, 1911
920 Elmwood Avenue, Joel A. Holmgren, 1911

Charles R. Ayars. Jeannie Lord Ayars house, 1420 Davis Street, 1899.
(All photographs in Appendix A are by Jenny Thompson.)

FREDERICK H. BAUMANN (1826-1921)
JEREMIAH KIERSTED CADY (1855-1925)
FRANK W. HANDY

Baumann was born in Germany and came to the United States about 1850. In 1856 he went into practice with Edward Burling; their firm was one of those that helped rebuild Chicago after the 1871 fire. Among their works were the Bryan Block, the Marine Building, the first Ashland block, the Crosby Opera House, Union National Bank, and the Metropolitan Block. Cady studied architecture at Cornell University and in Europe. He was one of the many young architects who began their careers working in the office of Burnham & Root. In 1887 he formed a partnership with Frank W. Handy that lasted until 1909, although Frederick Baumann was also his partner from 1889 to 1891. Among the buildings that Cady worked on were the Teutonic Building, the 7 North LaSalle Street Building, the State Bank at Madison and Kedzie streets, and the Medical Arts Building in Omaha. Baumann & Cady also designed Kimball Hall, the Bordeaux Apartments, and the Imperial Hotel in Chicago.

J. K. CADY
1138 Sheridan Road, Hebert A. Thomas, 1890

BAUMANN & CADY
221 Dempster Street, Charles P. Wheeler, 1890
222 Burnham Place, Alice Bunker Stockham, 1890

HANDY & CADY
1501 Forest Avenue, Frank M. Elliot, 1887
200 Burnham Place, William Hudson Harper, 1893
1629 Judson Avenue, Thomas Creighton, 1894
1314 Forest Avenue, Albert R. Barnes, 1889
1123 Ridge Avenue, William H. Warren, 1901

Handy & Cady. William H. Warren house, 1123 Ridge Avenue, 1901.

MINARD LAFEVRE BEERS (1847-1918)
WILLIAM WILSON CLAY (1849-1926)
LLEWELLYN B. DUTTON (1860-1944)

Beers, the son of a builder who named him for the French architect and author Minard LaFevre, was born too early to receive formal architectural education in a college or university. His father taught him carpentry and he then became an apprentice in the office of Joseph Ireland, a Cleveland architect. After Beers came to Chicago in 1871 he worked for Otis L. Wheelock and in 1876 formed a partnership with Oscar Cobb. After they separated in 1877 he practiced alone until forming another firm with William W. Clay and Llewellyn B. Dutton in December 1890. Clay had been the partner of Otis L. Wheelock from 1876 to 1886.

BEERS CLAY & DUTTON
1100 Forest Avenue, Milton H. Wilson, 1896
1101 Forest Avenue, Milton H. Wilson, 1896

MINARD L. BEERS
2207 Colfax Street, Fred P. Kappelman, 1900-1901

Beers Clay & Dutton. Milton H. Wilson house, 1101 Forest Avenue, 1896.

Edgard Ovet Blake. Edgar Ovet Blake house, 2518 Central Park Avenue, 1923.

EDGAR OVET BLAKE (1866-1953)

Edgar Ovet Blake was born in Evanston and lived here most of his life. After studying at the Art Institute of Chicago and in Paris, he worked briefly for Stephen A. Jennings (q.v.) and then opened his own office. He had a very large residential practice, but also designed churches, apartments, and commercial buildings.

2110 Orrington Avenue, John A. Scott, 1898
2608 Orrington Avenue, Ole Johnson, 1900
2026 Orrington Avenue, Salon C. Bronson, 1903
2030 Orrington Avenue, John A. Scott, 1903
1119-21 Hinman Avenue, Hugh A. Ross, 1903
1011 Maple Avenue, Peter Randlev, 1903
2036 Orrington Avenue, Walter Dill Scott, 1905
2040 Orrington Avenue, John A. Scott, 1905
2320 Orrington Avenue, Ulysses S. Grant, 1905
2340 Orrington Avenue, Frederick C. Eiselin, 1905
1242 Asbury Avenue, J. S. Luchey, 1905-1906
2244 Orrington Avenue, Charles W. Spofford, 1906
629 Colfax Street, George O. Curme, 1907
1564 Asbury Avenue, Henry J. Wallingford, 1908
1139 Elmwood Avenue, Morris C. Ploshman, 1908
2121 Orrington Avenue, Addison B. Phipps, 1909
819 Judson Avenue, Willis H. Towne, 1910
2608 Park Place, Royal J. Whitlock, 1910
2736 Hartzell Street, Daniel W. Alle, 1911
2865 Sheridan Place, Harry E. Byram, 1912
648 Dartmouth Place, John T. Gascoigne, 1913
618 Colfax Street, Mary H. Bovee, 1915
624 Colfax Street, Arthur C. Burch, 1915
2404 Lincoln Street, Luther L. Miller, 1916
810 Ingleside Place, Ernst V. Anderson, 1916
629 Garrett Place, Ellen K. French, 1916
222 Orrington Avenue, James T. Fulker, 1921
625 Clinton Place, Katherine E. Vernon, 1923
2518 Central Park Avenue, Edgar Ovet Blake, 1923
720 Central Street, Harry E. Brookby, 1924
2525 Orrington Avenue, Christian J. Golee, 1924
1021 Colfax Street, Leroy H. Sargent, 1925
2733 Lincoln Street, Howell N. Tyson, Jr., 1925
2400 Ewing Avenue, B. C. Burnham, 1926
3005 Colfax Street, John C. McGuire, 1931

DANIEL HUDSON BURNHAM (1846-1912)
JOHN WELLBORN ROOT (1850-1892)

1558 Ridge Avenue, George S. Lord, 1883*
1462 Ridge Avenue, George Watson Smith, 1883

231 Dempster Street, Clara Woodyatt, 1883 (refuted)
1403 Maple Avenue, Towner K. Webster, 1884 (annecdotal)
1620 Ridge Avenue, Thomas Lord, 1885*
316 Davis Street, Hugh Wilson, 1887*
Sherman Avenue and Church Street, Haven School, 1888*
600-612 Dempster Street, Arthur Orr Flats, 1889
355 Ridge Avenue, P.J. Kasper, 1889*
217 Dempster Street, William Brown, 1890
1401 Oak Street, Emmanuel Methodist Episcopal Church, 1890
1305 Forest Avenue, Charles Fuller, 1890
927 Noyes Street, Noyes Street School, 1892
318-20 Dempster Street, William Brown and H.R. Post, 1892
Crain Street and Oak Avenue, Crain Street (Larimer) School, 1894*
2645 Sheridan Road, Charles Deering, 1894*
1427 Chicago Avenue, First Presbyterian Church, 1894
425 Dempster Street, Hinman Avenue (Miller) School, 1898
Fisk Hall, Northwestern Preparatory School, 1899
232 Dempster Street, Tea House and Wall, 1909

* Demolished

Daniel Burnham lived in Evanston at 232 Dempster Street from 1886 until his death. Ironically, he did not build the house in which he lived. He remodeled the house over the years and added a tea house and concrete retaining wall that still stand. Some sources list the house in which his sister, Clara Woodyatt, lived as having been built by Burnham, although this has been refuted. Most of the houses Burnham designed in Evanston were for his personal friends. He was an active member of the community and belonged to several local clubs and organizations. When his wife died in 1938, his sons Hubert and Daniel Jr. demolished his house and subdivided the lot on which it stood. Emmanuel Methodist Church is largely attributed to his partner, John Root.

Kris Hartzell, 2013

FRANK WILLIAM CAULEY (1898-1984)
Born in Chicago, the son of an engineer who worked for Samuel Insull, Frank Cauley "always wanted to be an architect." He graduated from Armour Institute of Technology in 1922. Before he received his license to practice architecture, he designed the Orrington Hotel for the developer Victor C. Carlson. For a time he worked with architect Earl Reed in restoring the office of the Secretary of State and became an expert on the Classical Revival in the Northwest Territory. He went into business on his own, practicing until the 1929 crash. To weather the financial storm, he attended Kent College of Law and received his LL.D. in 1938. In April 1969 the Illinois Institute of Technology awarded him a J.D.

2915 Colfax Street, Mary L. Anderson, 1925
1101 Colfax Street, Edward W. Lyons, 1926
1313 Chancellor Street, Richard J. Penny, 1940
1317 Chancellor Street, Richard J. Penny, 1961

Frank Cauley. Mary L. Anderson house, 2915 Colfax Street, 1925.

MELVILLE CLARKE CHATTEN (1873-1957)
CHARLES HERRICK HAMMOND (1882-1969)

Melville Chatten graduated from the University of Illinois and continued his studies in Paris in 1905 and 1906. Charles Hammond received his degree in architecture at the Armour Institute of Technology and also completed his studies in Paris after winning the Chicago Architectural Club's Traveling Scholarship. Chatten and Hammond were in partnership from 1907 to 1927, when Dwight H. Perkins (q.v.) joined their firm. In 1933 Hammond joined the sons of Daniel H. Burnham in a new partnership, Burnham Bros. & Hammond, while Chatten continued in practice alone. Hammond served as president of the American Institute of Architects from 1928 to 1930 and as Supervising Architect of the State of Illinois from 1929 to 1936.

CHATTEN & HAMMOND
1101 Ridge Avenue, Horace White Armstrong, 1911
1010 Sheridan Road, John Builder, 1911
1030 Ridge Avenue, Frank H. Armstrong, 1912
208 Hamilton Street, Edward M. Skinner, 1913
147 Dempster Street, George Haskell, 1914
2756 Euclid Park Place, James S. Winn, 1918

Chatten & Hammond. Frank H. Armstrong house, 1030 Ridge Avenue, 1912.

FRANK A. CHILDS (1875-1965)
WILLIAM JONES SMITH (1881-1958)

Childs, a native Evanstonian, studied architecture at Armour Institute of Technology and from 1905 to 1907 at the Atelier Umbdenstock in Paris. Smith received degrees in architecture from the University of Pennsylvania in 1903 and the Ecole des Beaux Arts in 1907. He spent two years working for Cass Gilbert and three in the office of Holabird & Roche before forming a partnership with Childs in 1912. They designed schools and banks throughout the Midwest. In Evanston they designed the Mather Home (demolished), Nichols Middle School, Haven Middle School, St. Mary's School, and the second State National Bank Building (demolished).

CHILDS & SMITH
629 Noyes Street, Joseph Pearson, 1912
727 Clinton Place, Thomas B. Carson, 1912
731 Clinton Place, Thomas B. Carson, 1912
802 Clinton Place, Herbert H. Smith, 1915
815 Ridge Terrace, Childs Estate, 1915
823 Ridge Terrace, Childs Estate, 1915
829 Ridge Terrace, Childs Estate, 1915

Childs & Smith. Herbert H. Smith house, 802 Clinton Place, 1915.

H. RING CLAUSON (1890-1945)

The son of a plumbing contractor, H. Ring Clauson grew up in Evanston. He remodeled many houses, specializing in the Colonial Revival style, popular because of the rebuilding of Colonial Williamsburg.

1243 Forest Avenue, H. Ring Clauson, 1937
2501 Marcy Avenue, Gordon Copeland, 1937
2500 McDaniel Avenue, Lawrence Kempf, 1939
722 Sheridan Road, John W. Champion, 1940

H. Ring Clauson, Gordon Copeland house, 1243 Forest Avenue, 1937.

ROBERT SEELY DEGOLYER (1876-1952)
WALTER THAW STOCKTON (1895- 1989)

DeGolyer was Evanston born and bred. After studying a year at Yale, he attended the Massachusetts Institute of Technology, graduating in 1898. From 1902 to 1905 he was a designer in the office of John H. Parkinson in Los Angeles. He returned to Chicago in 1905 to be in charge of the office of Marshall & Fox. In 1915 he started his own firm and from 1923 to 1943 was in partnership with Walter Stockton. Their practice consisted mainly of residences, apartment buildings, and hotels, including the Barry Apartments and the Ambassador East Hotel in Chicago and the North Shore Hotel, the 923-25 Michigan Avenue apartments, and the 800-812 Michigan Avenue Apartments in Evanston.

ROBERT S. DEGOLYER
2767 Sheridan Road, Hugh W. McLean, 1919
2703 Euclid Park Place, Andrew K. Rodgers, 1919
2769 Sheridan Road, Lorne A. Griffin, 1920
2703 Colfax Street, Lowry Grulee, 1921
2757 Ridge Avenue, Walter M. Bond, 1921
2751 Ridge Avenue, Cary D. Terrell, 1921
2747 Ridge Avenue, J. D. W. Archer, 1921
1918 Sheridan Road, William G. Alexander, 1922
1624 Ashland Avenue, Franklin Bliss Snyder, 1922

DEGOLYER & STOCKTON
1038 Sheridan Road, T. C. Keller, 1925

Robert S. DeGolyer. Andrew K. Rodgers house, 2703 Euclid Park Place, 1919.

WILLOUGHBY JAMES EDBROOKE (1843-1896)
FRANKLIN PIERCE BURNHAM (1853-1909)

Willoughby J. Edbrooke, who was born in Deerfield, Illinois, was trained in the architectural profession by his father who was a contractor. After working for several Chicago architects, he went into practice with his brothers. He served as Commissioner of Buildings under Mayor Roche. In partnership from 1880 to 1892 with Franklin Burnham, Edbrooke worked on many courthouses throughout the state. In 1880 their firm won the national competition to design the Georgia Capitol in Atlanta. In 1891 Edbrooke was named Supervising Architect of the Treasury Department under President Benjamin Harrison and supervised the construction of the government buildings at the 1893 World's Columbian Exposition.

Franklin P. Burnham came to Chicago about 1876 and lived in the suburb of Kenilworth for a number of years, where he designed a great many houses and the Chicago North Western Railroad station. In later years he moved to Los Angeles where he continued his practice. In Evanston the firm of Edbrooke & Burnham designed the Wesley Avenue School, which once stood on the site of the present Dewey Elementary School.

EDBROOKE & BURNHAM
1432 Forest Avenue, David S. Cook 1883
1028 Greenwood Street, Edwin Hinchliffe, 1883
1022 Greenwood Street, George B. Dunham, 1883
1456 Ridge Avenue, John B. Kirk, 1884-85
1214 Maple Avenue, Joseph M. Larimer, 1885

FRANKLIN P. BURNHAM
1801 Asbury Avenue, Edward P. Prickett, 1895
1807 Asbury Avenue, Frank S. Davis, 1895
1228 Forest Avenue, William H. Burnet, 1897
1726 Ridge Avenue, E. C. Ray, 1898

Edbrooke & Burnham. George B. Dunham house, 1022 Greenwood Street, 1883.

JOHN J. FLANDERS (1848-1914)
WILLIAM CARBYS ZIMMERMAN (1859-1932)
ALBERT MOORE SAXE (1888-1953)
RALPH WALDO ZIMMERMAN

John J. Flanders began his career as a draughtsman for Burling & Adler. Briefly in partnership with Charles Furst, he was appointed architect to the Chicago Board of Education, serving eight years. He formed a partnership in 1886 with W. Carbys Zimmerman that lasted until 1898. Zimmerman maintained his practice alone until admitting his son-in-law, Albert M. Saxe, and his son, Ralph W. Zimmerman, to partnership.

FLANDERS & ZIMMERMAN
1100 Ridge Avenue, Anna Rew Gross, 1897

W. CARBYS ZIMMERMAN
1128 Ridge Avenue, Henry C. Rew, 1898
1100 Oak Avenue, Anna Rew Gross, 1901
1106 Oak Avenue, Anna Rew Gross, 1901
1133 Asbury Avenue, John Schwender, 1901
1139 Sheridan Road, Charles B. Hill, 1908
2829 Sheridan Place, Edward K. Warren, 1911

ZIMMERMAN SAXE & ZIMMERMAN
628 Colfax Street, David Beaton, 1916
1110 Ridge Avenue, Anna Rew Gross, 1925

Flanders & Zimmerman. Anna Rew Gross house, 1100 Ridge Avenue, 1897.

JOHN REED FUGARD (1886-1968)
GEORGE ARNOLD KNAPP (1888-)

John Reed Fugard was born in Newton, Iowa. He received his architectural degree from the University of Illinois in 1910 and began his practice in Chicago. Until 1925 he was in partnership with George A. Knapp, but then joined with Frederick J. Thielbar. Both firms specialized in apartments and hotels in the Chicago area.

FUGARD & KNAPP
806 Clinton Place, John Reed Fugard, 1920
810 Clinton Place, Jay Twitchell, 1921
2744 Ridge Avenue, Alf I. Bushnell, 1925

Fugard & Knapp. John Reed Fugard house, 806 Clinton Place, 1920.

WALTER BURLEY GRIFFIN (1876-1937)

Griffin, a graduate of the University of Illinois, was one of the most distinguished members of the Prairie School and worked for Frank Lloyd Wright in his Oak Park studio. Here he met Marion Mahony (1871-1961), the only woman architect of the Prairie School; they married in 1911. Griffin emphasized landscape planning and the integration of the structure into the landscape. In 1912 he won the international competition for the design of Australia's new capital, Canberra. His practice was centered in Australia and India for the rest of his life.

1710 Asbury Avenue, Mary H. Bovee, 1908
2740 Ridge Avenue, William Sinclair Lord, 1908
1024 Judson Avenue, Elsie Carter, 1910
1631 Ashland Avenue, Hurd Comstock, 1911-12
1416 Church Street, Hurd Comstock, 1911-12

Walter Burley Griffin. Mary H. Bovee house, 1710 Asbury Avenue, 1908.

LAWRENCE GUSTAVE HALLBERG (1844-1915)
MEYER JOSEPH STURM (1872-1954)
LAWRENCE GUSTAVE HALLBERG, JR. (1887-1971)
A well-known architect and a longtime resident of Evanston, the elder Hallberg was born and educated in Sweden. After working in the office of Sir Digby Wyatt in London, he came to the United States in 1877. From 1900 to 1902 he was in partnership with Meyer J. Sturm, who graduated from the Massachusetts Institute of Technology in 1896. The younger Hallberg studied architecture at Cornell University, graduating in 1910. In 1913 he became a partner in his father's firm and upon his father's death succeeded him as head of the company. In addition to residences, the elder Hallberg designed the Swedish Theological Seminary, which was moved from the lakefront, and later served as the main building of Kendall College.

HALLBERG & STURM
1030 Forest Avenue, Charles M. Putnam, 1901

LAWRENCE G. HALLBERG, JR.
1001 Sheridan Road, Sarah L. Vail, 1915
1005 Sheridan Road, Lawrence G. Hallberg, Jr., 1916
719 Milburn Street, Thomas F. Leahy, 1923
621 Ingleside Place, Samuel Crane Vail, 1926

Hallberg & Sturm. Charles M. Putnam house, 1030 Forest Avenue, 1902.

GEORGE LYONS HARVEY (1866-1923)
George Lyons Harvey, who was born in Chicago, graduated from the Massachusetts Institute of Technology in 1889 with a B.S. in Mechanical Engineering. After gaining experience in some of the large architectural firms, he started his own practice about 1893-94. He designed residences, factories, commercial buildings, as well as the first building of Evanston Hospital on Ridge Avenue.

1124 Judson Avenue, Charles L. Drain, 1896
1126 Michigan Avenue, William F. Hypes, 1897
1027 Sheridan Road, Frances M. Erwin, 1898
1616 Forest Place, Charles G. Ward, 1902

George Lyons Harvey. Charles G. Ward house, 1616 Forest Place, 1902.

WILLIAM HOLABIRD (1845-1923)
MARTIN ROCHE (1855-1927)

One of Chicago's most important architects, William Holabird was born in New York and graduated from the military academy at West Point. However, when his family moved to Chicago after the 1871 Chicago fire, he decided to become an architect and entered the office of William LeBaron Jenney. There he met Martin Roche with whom he formed a partnership in 1880, the beginnings of a firm that has continued in operation over a hundred and thirty years. (It is now known as Holabird & Root.) William Holabird moved to Evanston in the 1880s and built a home for his family at 1500 Oak Avenue. The firm of Holabird & Roche, famous for the skyscrapers they designed, also designed a number of residences in Evanston, as well as Fayerweather Hall at Northwestern University (demolished), the Evanston City Hall that once stood on Fountain Square, the Evanston Club that once stood at the northwest corner of Chicago Avenue and Grove street, and St. Mark's Episcopal Church.

HOLABIRD & ROCHE
1422 Judson Avenue, Frank K. Stevens, 1890
1225 Judson Avenue, Edwin A. Dawson, 1890
1110 Michigan Avenue, Robert S. Clark, 1890
1209-17 Maple Avenue, William Blanchard, 1892
2878 Sheridan Place, W. Gifford Jones, 1915
1601 Wesley Avenue, Louis A. Ferguson, 1915

Holabird & Roche. Frank K. Stevens house, 1422 Judson Avenue, 1890.

MYRON HUNT (1868-1952)

Hunt graduated from the Massachusetts Institute of Technology, where he and Dwight Perkins were friends. After Hunt came to Chicago, he shared offices with Perkins, Robert C. Spencer, Jr., and Frank Lloyd Wright in Steinway Hall. Hunt moved to Evanston in 1895 and designed both single family residences and double houses, popular in the nineteenth century, as well as apartment buildings. In 1903 he moved to California, where he continued a successful practice and was elected president of the California Chapter of the American Institute of Architects. Among his later works are the Rose Bowl, the Huntington Hartford Library, both in Pasadena, and the Los Angeles Civic Center.

1731 Wesley Avenue, Charles A. Wightman, 1895
1627 Wesley Avenue, Myron Hunt, 1896
1600-1602 Ashland Avenue, Harvey B. Hurd, 1896
1580 Ashland Avenue-1502 Davis Street, Harvey B. Hurd, 1897
1320 Lyons Street, Thomas Daley, 1897
1621 Wesley Avenue, Arthur S. Van Deusen, 1897
1414 Church Street, George R. Jenkins, 1897
1307-13 Ridge Avenue, Catherine White, 1897
1041 Judson Avenue, John W. Sweet, 1897
1045 Judson Avenue, John W. Sweet, 1897
930 Michigan Avenue, John E. Nolan, 1898
1228 Oak Avenue, William G. Sherer, 1898
1217 Ridge Avenue, Chancellor Livingston Jenks, Jr., 1898
1330 Church Street, John Taylor Pirie, Jr., 1898
1827 Asbury Avenue, John R. Woodbridge, 1898
1570-74 Ashland Avenue, Harvey B. Hurd, 1898
1401 Davis Street, Harlow N. Higinbotham, 1898-99
1606 Wesley Avenue, Harlow N. Higinbotham, 1898-99
1411-15 Davis Street, Harlow N. Higinbotham, 1898-99
1032-34 Michigan Avenue, Nina Drain, 1899
2512 Hartzell Street, Charles Nichols, 1899
1400-1404 Judson Avenue, W. M. Scott, 1899
1140 Forest Avenue, James A. Lawrence, 1899
815-17 Monroe Street, Michael L. O'Malia, 1901

Myron Hunt. Harvey B. Hurd double house, 1600-1602 Ashland Avenue, 1896.

JOHN THOMPSON WILSON JENNINGS

John T. Wilson Jennings arrived in Evanston about 1892. He started with an office in Chicago, but centered his practice in Evanston from 1896 to 1898. He designed Lincoln School that once stood on Main Street and the Rood Building that once stood on Fountain Square. By 1900 he moved to Madison, Wisconsin.

1023 Maple Avenue, A.L. Currey, 1894
1225 Michigan Avenue, Eugene E. Osborn, 1894
1048 Forest Avenue, William Dixon Marsh, 1894
1031 Sheridan Road, Charles S. Hannan, 1895
1142 Judson Avenue, Frank A. Warner, 1896

John T. Wilson Jennings. Charles S. Hannan house, 1031 Sheridan Road, 1895.

STEPHEN ALSTON JENNINGS (1857-1930)

A graduate of the University of Illinois, Stephen A. Jennings was the busiest architect in Evanston from 1885 to 1897. According to the newspapers, "his patrons find his work very satisfactory." He designed pretentious and elaborate homes for the wealthy. In 1899 he moved to Seattle, Washington, where he continued his practice; about 1912-13 he moved to Detroit. In addition to the many residences that he designed in Evanston, he was also the architect of St. Mary's Roman Catholic Church and the Bethlehem Lutheran Church that once stood at the southwest corner of Wesley Avenue and Greenwood Street.

1231 Maple Avenue, Jerome A. Smith, 1889
1200 Judson Avenue, S. Frank Wilson, 1889
1232 Judson Avenue, Frank A. Warner, 1889
1825 Asbury Avenue, Elia Gilbert Williams, 1890
1810-12 Chicago Avenue, Robert M. Hatfield, 1890
1426 Hinman Avenue, Mrs. J. H. Bayliss, 1890
1401-1407 Elmwood Avenue, Thomas Craven, 1890
1114 Judson Avenue, Chester P. Walcott, 1892
1109-11 Hinman Avenue, Edward S. Taylor, 1892

1404 Asbury Avenue, Thomas H. Beebe, 1892
2681 Sheridan Road, H. K. Snider, 1893
732 Madison Street, Nicholas Treff, 1893
1560 Oak Avenue, John W. Low, 1893
1235-37 Judson Avenue, William Blanchard, 1893
1143 Forest Avenue, James W. Donnell, 1893
1015 Hinman Avenue, Stephen F. ReQua, 1894
1236 Judson Avenue, Frank A. Warner, 1894
1232 Ridge Avenue, William Hugh Jones, 1894
416 Greenwood Street, Henry A. Freeman, 1894
1710 Wesley Avenue, Sarah S. Linsley, 1894
1334 Asbury Avenue, Milton L. Record, 1895
1817 Asbury Avenue, Sarah E. Hatch, 1895
413-15 Dempster Street, Mrs. J. C. Dyke, 1896

Stephen A. Jennings. James W. Donnell house, 1143 Forest Avenue, 1893.

ARTHUR HOWELL KNOX (1881-1973)

Knox, who was born in Topeka, Kansas, but lived in Evanston most of his life, was educated at Armour Institute of Technology. He went into practice in 1904 and was briefly in partnership with Clarence Hatzfeld. During the 1930s he worked for various federal agencies in design and construction. His practice ranged from simple, unpretentious bungalows to his most notable building in Evanston, the Levere Memorial Temple.

2400 Park Place, Arthur Howell Knox, 1911
2522 Hartzell Street, Walter Hardy, 1912
2714 Hartzell Street, Samuel Gilbert, 1916
732 Sheridan Road, Frank Milhening, 1920
917 Edgemere Court, Antonin Sterba, 1922
2721 Hartzell Street, Carl A. Bessey, 1923
2721 Harrison Street, Samuel H. Gilbert, 1925
2221 Lincolnwood Drive, Amelia Jacobson, 1925
2425 Hartzell Street, J. William Link, 1927

Arthur Howell Knox. Arthur Howell Knox house, 2400 Park Place, 1911.

JOSIAH CARSON LANE

Josiah Carson Lane, who had started his practice in Chicago by 1884, moved to Evanston about 1892 and had an office here. He moved to Florida in 1898.

1203-1205 Hinman Avenue-425 Hamilton Street, Orvis French, 1892
1211-13 Judson Avenue, Mary E. Scranton, 1892
1304 Judson Avenue, Mrs. J. C. Dyke, 1893
1847-49 Asbury Avenue, Charles J. Gilbert, 1893
1217 Michigan Avenue, William L. Wells, 1894
1735 Wesley Avenue, Charles A. Wightman 1894
2103 Orrington Avenue, Mary Stevens, 1895
423 Greenleaf Street, Charles K. Ober, 1895
427 Greenleaf Street, Charles K. Ober, 1895
1042 Michigan Avenue, Mrs. Erasmus O. Hills, 1895
1046 Michigan Avenue, William E. Hills, 1895
1721 Wesley Avenue, Charles A. Wightman, 1896
1745 Wesley Avenue, Charles A. Wightman, 1897

Josiah Carson Lane. William L. Wells house, 1217 Michigan Avenue, 1894.

ELMO CAMERON LOWE (1876-1933)
JOHN CARLISLE BOLLENCACHER (1884-1939)
ALFRED HOYT GRANGER (1867-1939)

Born in Illinois, Elmo C. Lowe graduated from the Massachusetts Institute of Technology in 1905 and worked first as a designer for Bertram Goodhue. From 1908 to 1924 he was in partnership with John C. Bollenbacher, who also attended M.I.T. In 1924 Alfred Granger, an 1887 graduate of M.I.T., joined the firm. After Lowe's retirement in 1930, Granger and Bollenbacher continued the practice. They designed churches, college buildings, and residences throughout the Midwest, including the First Evangelical Church, Chicago; Bryn Mawr Community Church, Chicago; the Chicago Club; the Cloisters Apartments, Chicago; St. John's Lutheran Church, Wilmette; and Methodist churches in Wilmette and Berwyn.

LOWE & BOLLENBACHER
715 Sheridan Road, Lillian E. Raymond, 1910
2206 Orrington Avenue, Mrs. M. J. Eastman, 1912
625 Haven Street, F. K. Jackson, 1914
2501 Colfax Street, Elmo C. Lowe, 1916
2218 Orrington Avenue, Harold J. Clark, 1919
2609 Lincoln Street, Sidney J. Williams, 1919
2000 Sheridan Road, Frank O' Beck, 1921
2910 Harrison Street, Gilbert L. Campbell, 1923
2516 Lincoln Street, Frederick H. Pattee, 1923

GRANGER LOWE & BOLLENBACHER
630 Dartmouth Place, Hugh W. McCulloch, 1925
625 Library Place, Arthur Guy Terry, 1925
2447 Lincolnwood Drive, Justus P. Bauer, 1926
2525 Colfax Street, William J. Mauer, 1926
2411 Central Park Avenue, Olin A. Wakeman, 1926
3030 Grant Street, James E. Miller, 1927

Lowe & Bollenbacher. Sidney J. Williams house, 2609 Lincoln Street, 1919.

ASA LYON (1849- ?)

Lyon came to Chicago from Boston where he worked in the office of Cummings & Sears. Generally considered Evanston's first resident architect, he actually lived in South Evanston from 1872 to 1875, where it was said, he designed some houses for the developers Warren & Keeney. However, Lyon returned to Chicago after 1875 and then left the Chicago area entirely until 1881, when he set up an office in Evanston and had a very active architectural practice until he left for Grand Rapids, Michigan, in 1884.

215 Lake Street, Michael Tiernan, 1881
1314 Hinman Avenue, Eunice Clarinda Reed, 1882
1454 Asbury Avenue, Nelson B. Record, 1882
1335 Asbury Avenue, Charles Comstock, 1882
1250 Asbury Avenue (moved from 1224 Greenwood Street in 1910), Charles Comstock, 1882.

Asa Lyon. Eunice Clarinda Reed house, 1314 Hinman Avenue, 1882.

GEORGE WASHINGTON MAHER (1864-1926)

A West Virginian by birth, Maher was one of the architects of the Prairie School who sought to define an American architectural idiom. He was a resident of Kenilworth and designed many houses there. He was an apprentice in the office of Bauer & Hill and then worked for Joseph Lyman Silsbee (q.v.), where he met Frank Lloyd Wright. He completed his education in 1893 with a year in Europe studying and sketching; he started his practice after his marriage in 1894. In addition to residences in Evanston, he designed the University Building for Charles A. Wightman and the first Patten Gymnasium (demolished) and Swift Hall of Engineering for Northwestern University.

1714 Asbury Avenue, Charles Richardson, 1904
1019 Michigan Avenue, Thomas B. Carson, 1904
1023 Michigan Avenue, Thomas B. Carson, 1909
1022 Michigan Avenue, Thomas B. Carson, 1909
624 Central Street, Betsy A. Bridge, 1909
635 Milburn Street, Betsy A. Bridge, 1909
2505 Orrington Avenue, Betsy A. Bridge, 1909

1583 Ashland Avenue, Eda Hurd Lord, 1909
1421 Elinor Place, Eda Hurd Lord, 1909
310 Church Street, A. D. Sheridan, 1910
1575 Ashland Avenue, George S. Lord, 1911
1314 Ridge Avenue, George B. Dryden, 1916
1050 Hinman Avenue, Mark C. Rasmussen, 1917

George W. Maher. Eda Hurd Lord house, 1583 Ashland Avenue, 1909.

ERNEST ALFRED MAYO (1868-1946)
PETER B. MAYO (1895-1976)

Ernest A. Mayo was born in England and worked in the office of H. M. Townsend in Birmingham. After practicing briefly in South Africa, he came to Chicago and served as an architectural advisor for the construction division of the 1893 World's Columbian Exposition and designed several of the administration buildings. Ernest Mayo, who dominated the design of residential architecture in Evanston from the turn of the century until his death in 1946, was responsible for many houses for wealthy businessmen and professionals; he also remodeled a great many of the early houses in town. His son Peter graduated from Yale University in 1917 and from the Ecole d' Artillerie at Fountainebleau in 1918, after which he became a partner in his father's successful firm.

ERNEST A. MAYO
1122 Judson Avenue, John M. Thomas, 1894
1225 Forest Avenue, Charles H. Barry, 1899
1110 Maple Avenue, Nellie Dugdale 1899
2523 Harrison Street, Martha Mercer, 1899
1218 Sheridan Road, Frederick E. French, 1901
1225 Sheridan Road, Wallace R. Condict, 1902
1215 Forest Avenue, Everett H. Ball, 1902
1118 Sheridan Road, Achilles H. Reece, 1904
1203 Forest Avenue, George M. Ludlow, 1905
1022 Hinman Avenue, Mrs. E. E. Nafis, 1905
1217 Forest Avenue, George W. Clark, 1907
1637 Judson Avenue, Charles P. Whitney, 1908
1214 Forest Avenue, M. B. Austin, 1909
616 Central Street, Betsy A. Bridge, 1909

2735 Sheridan Road, Augusta V. Crawford, 1909
1233 Crain Street, Francis A. Hardy, 1909
2436 Orrington Avenue, Sherman C. Kingsley, 1909
1120 Forest Avenue, Ernest Reckitt, 1909
714 Milburn Street, Willard E. Hotchkiss, 1909
1210 Forest Avenue, Rollin Keyes, 1910
1025 Forest Avenue, Edwin Hurlbut, 1910
1030 Sheridan Road, Thomas Hair, 1911
115 Dempster Street, Chester Cook, 1911
1318 Forest Avenue, Frank S. Cunningham, 1911
133 Dempster Street, Ira Barton Cook, 1911
2726 Sheridan Road, Charles W. James, 1912
1110 Sheridan Road, Robert E. Wilsey, 1912
1117 Sheridan Road, Frank Parker Davis, 1912
101 Greenleaf Street, Henry Dawes, 1913
1046 Sheridan Road, Albert H. Williams, 1914
144 Greenwood Street, Robert L. Scott, 1915
1010 Michigan Avenue, Anson Mark, 1916

MAYO & MAYO
1000 Sheridan Road, John F. Trow, 1919
404 Church Street, Charles P. Whitney, 1919
2746 Euclid Park Place, Budd C. Corbus, 1922
2317 Central Park Avenue, John H. Platt, 1927
2750 Sheridan Road, Charles E. Mallers, 1927
900 Edgemere Court, Harry N. Selling, 1928

Mayo & Mayo. Charles E. Mallers house, 2750 Sheridan Road, 1927.

JOHN AUGUSTUS NYDEN (1878-1932)

John Nyden, who was born in Sweden, began his architectural practice in Chicago in 1907. A major during World War I, he supervised the construction of general and debarkation hospitals in the United States, acting as liaison officer between the construction division and the surgeon general's office. Later, in private practice he designed many residential hotels and apartment buildings, including the Admiral Hotel, the Commonwealth Hotel, the Fairfax Hotel, the Bethany Swedish Methodist Church, and the Builder & Merchants Bank in Chicago. In Evanston his firm designed the City National Bank (later remodeled for First National Bank), the Evanshire Hotel, the Hahn Building, and the Church Street Building. He was appointed Illinois State Architect in 1926.

2855 Sheridan Place, Oscar Haugan, 1911
1041 Michigan Avenue, John Somerville, 1916

John A. Nyden. Oscar Haugan house, 2855 Sheridan Place, 1911.

WILLIAM AUGUSTUS OTIS (1855-1929)

Born in New York, Otis studied architecture at the University of Michigan and completed his formal education at the Ecole des Beaux Arts in Paris. He came to Chicago in 1882 and began as a draughtsman in the office of William LeBaron Jenney. Otis was Jenney's partner from 1886 until 1889, when he opened his own firm. He practiced independently until he admitted Edwin Hill Clark to partnership in 1909; their association lasted until 1920. Otis, who lived in Winnetka, was well known for his designs of residences and libraries; he was also a lecturer at the Art Institute of Chicago. Among his works are Christ Church in Winnetka, the Municipal Tuberculosis Sanitarium in Chicago, the University Club in Evanston, and Lunt Hall and Music Hall on the Northwestern campus.

1232 Asbury Avenue, Clement Knowles Pittman, 1891-92
2016 Sheridan Road, Charles J. Little, 1893
1707 Hinman Avenue, Humphreys H. C. Miller, 1894
2203 Orrington Avenue, Northwestern University, 1895
1424 Judson Avenue, Thomas C. Clark, 1902

William A. Otis. Humphreys H. C. Miller house, 1707 Hinman Avenue, 1894.

DWIGHT HEALD PERKINS (1897-1941)
JOHN LEONARD HAMILTON (1878-1955)
WILLIAM KINNE FELLOWS (1870-1948)

A nationally known designer of educational buildings, Perkins studied at the Massachusetts Institute of Technology. In charge of the office of Burnham & Root while Burnham was busy with the 1893 World's Columbian Exposition, Perkins established his own office soon after the Fair in Steinway Hall, his first independent commission. He shared space with Robert C. Spencer, Jr., Myron Hunt, and Frank Lloyd Wright, with whose ideas he was much in sympathy. From 1905 to 1911 he was the architect for the Chicago Board of Education and designed approximately forty schools. A close friend of the landscape architect Jens Jensen, Perkins was active in promoting and designing the West Park System for Chicago and worked to establish the Cook County Forest Preserve System. He also served as the first president of the Chicago Regional Planning Association. He was in partnership with John Leonard Hamilton, who was educated at the Chicago Manual Training School, from 1905 to 1911, when William K. Fellows joined the firm. In 1927, in failing health, he formed a partnership with Melville Chatten and Charles Herrick Hammond, which lasted until his retirement in 1933.

DWIGHT H. PERKINS
2044 Sheridan Road, J. Scott Clark, 1901
2319 Lincoln Street, Dwight Heald Perkins, 1904

PERKINS & HAMILTON
2405 Lincoln Street, William A. Colledge, 1906
2333 Lincoln Street, Edwin F. Walker, 1908
1415 Elinor Place, Eda Hurd Lord, 1910
1416 Elinor Place, Eda Hurd Lord, 1910

PERKINS FELLOWS & HAMILTON
2610 Lincoln Street, Joseph H. Kearney, 1911
2700 Lincoln Street, Charles M. Fairchild, 1911
2212 Lincoln Street, Robert A. Worstall, 1912
1550 Ashland Avenue, Eda Hurd Lord, 1912
1133 Michigan Avenue, John E. Blunt, Jr., 1916

Perkins, Fellows & Hamilton. Joseph J. Kearney house, 2610 Lincoln Street, 1911.

LAWRENCE BRADFORD PERKINS (1907-1997)
EDWARD TODD WHEELER (1906-1987)
PHILIP WILL, JR. (1906-1985)
Lawrence B. Perkins, the son of architect Dwight H. Perkins, graduated from the College of Architecture of Cornell University in 1931. After working in the Chicago office of Howard T. Fisher's General House, Inc., he went into partnership in 1935 with another Cornell graduate, Philip Will, Jr. The following year E. Todd Wheeler joined the partnership, and the firm continued as Perkins, Wheeler & Will until 1944, when the name was changed to The Perkins & Will Partnership. In its early years the firm concentrated on residential and educational work, but it soon grew into one of the largest and most powerful architectural firms in the country. Because of Perkins' service to education, the American Association of School Administrators gave him the Distinguished Service Award for 1975. Perkins served for several years as chairman of the Evanston Plan Commission. After his retirement from active practice, he became an adjunct professor at the University of Illinois at Chicago Circle. In Evanston the firm of Perkins & Will designed the Methodist Building; Foster Fieldhouse; the Second Church of Christ, Scientist; the Harper & Row Building; Dawes School; Skiles Junior High School; Chute Junior High School; and additions to Evanston Township High School.

PERKINS, WHEELER & WILL
2949 Harrison Street, Philip Will, Jr., 1937
2501 McDaniel Avenue, Sidney J. Williams, 1938
2940 Harrison Street, Lawrence B. Perkins 1940

PERKINS & WILL
1550 Asbury Avenue, Methodist Church Board of Pensions, 1964
1560 Asbury Avenue, Methodist Church Board of Pensions, 1964
1610 Asbury Avenue, Methodist Church Board of Pensions, 1964

1616 Asbury Avenue, Methodist Church Board of Pensions, 1964
1311 Grove Street, Methodist Church Board of Pensions, 1964
1301 Davis Street, Methodist Church Board of Pensions, 1964
1311 David Street, Methodist Church Board of Pensions, 1964

Perkins Wheeler & Will. Lawrence B. Perkins house, 2940 Harrison Street, 1940.

WILLIAM C. POCKLINGTON (1851- ?)

Pocklington, who was born in England, came to the United States in 1852 with his parents. He learned the trade of carpenter in Waukegan and moved to Evanston in 1871. He worked with his father's company, the Northwestern Planing Mill, before starting his own contracting business seven years later. He continued to call himself an architect until 1905, despite the fact that the Illinois law licensing architects went into effect in 1897.

415 Greenwood Street, Charles H. Harbert, 1889
1411 Judson Avenue, Edward S. Turner, 1889
1139 Ridge Avenue, Gideon Kellogg, 1889
516-18 Greenwood Street, Edward W. Learned, 1889
1216 Judson Avenue, Thaddeus W. Heermans, 1890
1321 Elwood Avenue, Swan Anderson, 1893
1217 Lee Street, E. T. Richardson, 1893
1114 Grant Street, Mrs. John J. Foster, 1894
2127 Maple Avenue, Charles Beck, 1894
1940 Sheridan Road, F. W. Beers, 1894
1936 Orrington Avenue, Ellen E. Langlois, 1894
2106 Orrington Avenue, Arthur L. Currey, 1895
2111 Maple Avenue, Frank Hughes, 1895
1911 Colfax Street, J. B. Finch, 1895
1814 Wesley Avenue, Alexander Balfour, 1895
1512 Judson Avenue, Mary Scott, 1896
930 Maple Avenue, Adam Thompson, 1896
726 Monroe Street, Nicholas A. Kirschten, 1897
806 Monroe Street, John P. Risch, 1897

William C. Pocklington. Charles H. Harbert house, 415 Greenwood Street, 1889.

IRVING KANE POND (1857-1939)
ALLEN BARTLITT POND (1858-1929)

Irving K. Pond and Allen B. Pond were both born in Ann Arbor, Michigan, and both graduated from the University of Michigan. After working for S. S. Beman, they went into partnership in 1887. Although they were innovative designers and friends of the Prairie School architects, they are not considered members of the Prairie School. Irving K. Pond served as president of the American Institute of Architects in 1908. Among their well-known designs are two settlement houses in Chicago, Hull-House and Gads Hill; the Michigan Union Building at the University of Michigan; and Lorado Taft's studio at 60th Street and Ellis Avenue in Chicago.

POND & POND
225 Hamilton Street, Elliot Anthony, 1894
1800 Asbury Avenue, Charles M. Howe, 1897
1820 Asbury Avenue, LeRoy C. Noble, 1899
1425 Ridge Avenue (moved from 910 Greenwood Street), Volney W. Foster, 1900
1410 Asbury Avenue, Winifred A. Erickson, 1912
2706 Lincoln Street, Charles D. Marsh, 1913

Pond & Pond. Elliot Anthony house, 225 Hamilton Street, 1894.

HENRY RAEDER (? -1943)
ARTHUR S. COFFIN (1857-1938)
BENJAMIN S. CROCKER

Henry Raeder had offices in the late 1800s both in Chicago and Duluth, where he designed the Palladio Building and the Chamber of Commerce. About 1889 the firm of Raeder, Coffin & Crocker was formed and it lasted until 1895 when Crocker left. From 1896 to 1904 the firm continued as Raeder & Coffin, after which Raeder carried on alone. One of Raeder's most notable works was the sixteen-story east portion of the American Furniture Mart on Lake Shore Drive in Chicago. In Evanston he designed mostly residences plus Willard and Orrington schools. For many years he lived at 1745 Asbury Avenue (demolished).

RAEDER, COFFIN & CROCKER

1742 Asbury Avenue, Charles P. Mitchell, 1889-90
1733 Asbury Avenue, Charles Chandler, 1890-91
1104 Greenwood Streets, William O. Dean, 1892
2236 Orrington Avenue, Frank W. McCulloch, 1895

HENRY RAEDER

1509 Asbury Avenue, William J. Fabian, 1922

Raeder Coffin & Crocker. Charles P. Mitchell house, 1742 Asbury Avenue, 1889-90.

HOWARD VAN DOREN SHAW (1869-1926)

Born in Chicago, Shaw received his architectural training at Yale University and the Massachusetts Institute of Technology. He worked for Jenney & Mundie before setting up his own practice. He was well-known for his handsome and carefully detailed residential designs, especially in the Hyde Park area and Lake Forest. He also designed the Quadrangle Club at the University of Chicago, the University Church of Disciples of Christ, the Lakeside Press of R. R. Donnelley & Sons, McKinlock Court of the Art Institute of Chicago, the Goodman Theatre, and the charming center of Lake Forest, Market Square.

2233 Orrington Avenue, Carl E. Williams, 1909
1005 Michigan Avenue, Cyrus Mark, 1913
747 Sheridan Road, Harry A. Swigert, 1915
2856 Sheridan Place, William E. Hall, 1927

Howard Van Doren Shaw. Carl E. Williams house, 2233 Orrington Avenue, 1909.

JOSEPH LYMAN SILSBEE (1845-1913)

Born in Massachusetts, Silsbee earned an A.B. at Harvard University and then attended the Massachusetts Institute of Technology for three years. He practiced in Syracuse, New York, for ten years before moving to Chicago in 1882 where he formed a partnership with a Syracuse friend, Edward A. Kent. In 1884 the firm designed the interiors for the Potter Palmer mansion on Lake Shore Drive. After Kent returned east in 1890, Silsbee remained in practice in Chicago. Among those who worked in his office were Frank Lloyd Wright and George W. Maher. Silsbee designed many residences as well as the Illinois Bell Telephone Building at Franklin and Washington streets and the Garfield Park grandstand.

202 Greenwood Street, Arthur Orr, 1889
1625 Ashland Avenue, Harvey B. Hurd, 1890
235 Greenwood Street, William Hammond, 1892

Joseph Lyman Silsbee. Arthur Orr house, 202 Greenwood Street, 1889.

ROBERT CLOSSON SPENCER JR. (1864-1953)
HORACE SWETT POWERS (1872-1928)

A graduate of the Massachusetts Institute of Technology, Spencer also had a degree from the University of Wisconsin in mechanical engineering. Like many of his contemporaries he studied in

Europe for several years on a Rotch Traveling Fellowship. When he returned he worked for the Boston firm of Shepley, Rutan & Coolidge and later moved to their Chicago office. In 1894 Spencer collaborated with a young draughtsman, Robert R. Kendall, on a number of commissions. In 1895 Spencer opened his own office; two years later he moved into Steinway Hall with his friend Dwight H. Perkins. In 1905 Spencer formed a partnership with Horace S. Powers, who was a graduate of the Armour Institute of Technology; their partnership lasted until 1923. Spencer then became a professor at Oklahoma A. & M. College. While he was in Oklahoma he founded the Chicago Casement Hardware Company to manufacture and sell window opening devices. From 1930 to 1934 he was on the faculty of the University of Florida, during which time he also painted murals for the federal government.

ROBERT C. SPENCER, JR. & ROBERT R. KENDALL
617 Library Place, Northwestern University, 1894
1012 Lake Shore Boulevard, John Stanley Grepe, 1894

ROBERT C. SPENCER, JR.
1833 Asbury Avenue, William G. Hempstead, 1895
1743 Wesley Avenue, Charles A. Wightman, 1895
2444 Pioneer Road, Charles A. Wightman, 1895
2450 Pioneer Road, Charles A. Wightman, 1895
2454 Pioneer Road, Charles A. Wightman, 1895

SPENCER & POWERS
1201 Sheridan Road, Nathan Wilbur Williams, 1912
2425 Pioneer Road, William G. Leisenring, 1915

Spencer & Powers. Nathan Wilbur Williams house, 1201 Sheridan Road, 1912.

THOMAS EDDY TALLMADGE (1876-1940)
VERNON SPENCER WATSON (1879-1950)
Thomas Eddy Tallmadge graduated from the Massachusetts Institute of Technology in 1898. After a stint in the office D. H. Burnham & Company, he went to Europe in 1904 on a Chicago Architectural Club Traveling Fellowship. In 1905 he formed a partnership with Vernon S. Watson that lasted until 1936. Tallmadge was the architect of the Colonial Village at the 1933 Century of Progress Fair and he also served as a member of the Architectural Commission for the restoration of Colonial Williamsburg.

He also lectured on architectural history at the Art Institute of Chicago and taught at Armour Institute of Technology. He combined a career as a practicing architect and as an author of books and articles about architectural history.

TALLMADGE & WATSON
1112 Asbury Avenue, Quinlan & Tyson, 1906
926 Michigan Avenue, Edward H. Kimbark, 1906
633 Michigan Avenue (moved from 919 Judson Avenue in 1946), Chester O. Andrews, 1906
1315 Forest Avenue, Charles C. Linthicum, 1907-1908
1000 Forest Avenue, Frederick S. Kretsinger, 1908
1239 Asbury Avenue, Adelaide S. Ames, 1908
625 Milburn Street, K. R. Peck, 1908
1118 Oak Avenue, James Wigginton, 1908
1136 Lake Shore Boulevard, Wallace Condict, 1909
1114 Lake Shore Boulevard, Robert Marshal Roloson, 1909
2222 Lincoln Street, Charles M. Howe, 1909
2200 Lincoln Street, Harold G. Peterson, 1910
1000 Lake Shore Boulevard, Mrs. Edmund Adcock, 1911
1041 Ridge Avenue, Knowlton L. Ames, 1911
1045 Ridge Avenue, Knowlton L. Ames, 1911
1215 Greenleaf Street, Henry Hampton Kerr, 1912
1135 Judson Avenue, Carl S. Jefferson, 1912
1120 Asbury Avenue, Harry H. Mallory, 1912
1145 Sheridan Road, Carroll Shaffer, 1913
2246 Orrington Avenue, Robert K. Row, 1915
586 Ingleside Park, Daniel H. Boone, 1925
2870 Sheridan Place, Fred W. Sargent, 1926
2514 Marcy Avenue, Charlotte M. Heermans, 1927
2430 Orrington Avenue, Samuel J. Sackett, 1927

THOMAS E. TALLMADGE
2756 Ridge Avenue, Harry A. Paskind, 1938

Tallmadge & Watson. Charles M. Howe house, 2222 Lincoln Street, 1909.

JOHN SHELLETTE VAN BERGEN (1885-1969)

After growing up in Oak Park, the capital of Prairie School architecture, Van Bergen spent a year in California following his high school graduation and then came back to Chicago and worked in Walter Burley Griffin's Steinway Hall office. He took a three-month course at the Chicago Technical College in preparation for the architectural licensing examination. He then went to work for Frank Lloyd Wright with whom he remained until Wright closed his studio in 1909. He passed the architectural examination and received his license in 1911. After working for William Drummond, he started his own practice and had an office in Evanston in 1917-18 before settling in Ravinia at the south end of Highland Park. From 1955 to 1968 he practiced architecture in Santa Barbara, California.

741 Sheridan Road, Harold R. White, 1915
1026 Michigan Avenue, George S. Ballard, 1915

John S. Van Bergen. George S. Ballard house, 1026 Michigan Avenue, 1915.

CHESTER HOWE WALCOTT (1883-1947)
RUSSELL SMITH WALCOTT (1889- 1959)
EDWIN HILL CLARK (1899-1967)
ARTHUR G. BROWN (1869-1934)

Chester Howe Walcott and his brother Russell grew up in Evanston. Chester earned a B.S. at Princeton University and then traveled extensively in France and Italy. From 1912 to 1917 he was in partnership with Arthur G. Brown; from 1919 to 1920 with his brother; and from 1920 to 1922 with Edwin Hill Clark; after which he practiced alone. Edwin Clark had been the partner of William A. Otis (q.v.) from 1909 to 1920.

BROWN & WALCOTT
1103 Sheridan Road, Edwin Sherman, 1912
1120 Lake Shore Boulevard, Mrs. Kenneth Barnhart, 1914

CHESTER H. WALCOTT
2864 Sheridan Place, Charles J. Trayner, 1919
124 Greenleaf Street, Clifford Off, 1919
1501 Asbury Avenue, William G. Burt, 1919
1020 Lake Shore Boulevard, William R. Johnston, 1920

CLARK & WALCOTT
2510 Lincoln Street, James Roy Ozanne, 1922
1000 Maple Avenue, John B. Ortlund, Jr., 1922

RUSSELL S. WALCOTT
583 Ingleside Place, Johnston A. Bowman, 1928

Chester H. Walcott. William G. Bart house, 1501 Asbury Avenue, 1919.

HARRY BERGEN WHEELOCK (1861-1934)

Harry Bergen Wheelock was born in Galesburg. After the death of his father, George Bergen, he was adopted by the architect Otis L. Wheelock. He studied civil engineering but left college before graduating to take over Wheelock's architectural practice. H. B. Wheelock was active in the establishment of the Chicago Architectural Club and the Illinois Society of Architects, as well as the Architectural Registration Act in Illinois. His most noteworthy design was the Methodist Book Concern Building on Washington Street in Chicago; he also designed Covenant Methodist Church in Evanston.

1225 Ridge Avenue, Charles G. Neely, 1897
1112 Greenwood Street, David R. Forgan, 1899
1028 Hinman Avenue, H. W. Rogers, 1899
1032 Hinman Avenue, H. W. Rogers, 1899
1115 Hinman Avenue, Mrs. Percy Palmer, 1904
617 Dartmouth Place, Adam E. Dunn, 1909
627 Dartmouth Place, John Brunner, 1909

Harry Bergen Wheelock. David R. Forgan house, 1112 Greenwood Street, 1899.

Appendix B

Architectural Index By Address

Compiled by Kris Hartzell, with the assistance of Hayley Helms and Hannah Van Loon

1112 Asbury Ave.	Tallmadge & Watson	Quinlan & Tyson	1906
1117 Asbury Ave.	Charles Ayars	Allen A. Keene	1903
1120 Asbury Ave.	Tallmadge & Watson	Harry H. Mallory	1912
1133 Asbury Ave.	W. Carbys Zimmerman	John Schwender	1901
1145 Asbury Ave.	Charles Ayars	Edward B. Griswald	1897
1232 Asbury Ave.	William Otis	Clement Knowles Pittman	1891-92
1239 Asbury Ave.	Tallmadge & Watson	Adelaide S. Amcs	1908
1242 Asbury Ave.	Edgar Ovet Blake	J.S. Luchey	1905-06
1250 Asbury Ave.	Asa Lyon	Charles Comstock	1882
1334 Asbury Ave.	Stephen Jennings	Milton L. Record	1895
1335 Asbury Ave.	Asa Lyon	Charles Comstock	1882
1404 Asbury Ave.	Stephen Jennings	Thomas H. Beebe	1892
1410 Asbury Ave.	Pond & Pond	Winifred A. Erickson	1912
1454 Asbury Ave.	Asa Lyon	Nelson B. Record	1882
1501 Asbury Ave.	Chester Wolcott	William G. Burt	1919
1509 Asbury Ave.	Henry Raeder	Williams J. Fabian	1922
1550 Asbury Ave.	Perkins & Will	Methodist Church Board of Pensions	1964
1550 Asbury Ave.	Perkins & WIll	Eda Hurd Lord	1912
1560 Asbury Ave.	Perkins & Will	Methodist Church Board of Pensions	1964
1564 Asbury Ave.	Edgar Ovet Blake	Henry J. Walingford	1908
1610 Asbury Ave.	Perkins & Will	Methodist Church Board of Pensions	1964
1616 Asbury Ave.	Perkins & Will	Methodist Church Board of Pensions	1964
1710 Asbury Ave.	Walter Griffin	Mary H. Bovee	1908
1714 Asbury Ave.	George W. Maher	Charles Richardson	1904
1719 Asbury Ave.	Charles Ayars	Eliza J. Hinsdale	1894
1733 Asbury Ave.	Raeder, Coffin, & Crocker	Charles Chandler	1890-91
1742 Asbury Ave.	Raeder, Coffin, & Crocker	Charles P. Mitchell	1889-90
1800 Asbury Ave.	Pond & Pond	Charles M. Howe	1897
1801 Asbury Ave.	Franklin Burnham	Edward P. Prickett	1895
1807 Asbury Ave.	Franklin Burnham	Frank S. Davis	1895
1809 Asbury Ave.	Charles Ayars	George R. Work	1898
1817 Asbury Ave.	Stephen Jennings	Sarah E. Hatch	1895
1820 Asbury Ave.	Pond & Pond	LeRoy C. Noble	1889
1825 Asbury Ave.	Stephen Jennings	Elia Gilbert Williams	1890
1827 Asbury Ave.	Myron Hunt	John R. Woodridge	1898
1833 Asbury Ave.	Robert Spencer Jr.	William G. Hempstead	1895

1847-49 Asbury Ave.	Josiah Lane	Charles J. Gilbert	1893
1619 Ashland Ave.	Charles Ayars	Henry S. Shedd	1910
1624 Ashland Ave.	Robert S. Degoyler	Franklin Bliss Snyder	1922
1570-74 Ashland Ave	Myron Hunt	Harvey B. Hurd	1898
1575 Ashland Ave	George W. Maher	George S. Lord	1911-12
1580 Ashland Ave	Myron Hunt	Harvey B. Hurd	1897
1583 Ashland Ave	George W. Maher	Eda Hurd Lord	1909
1600-02 Ashland Ave	Myron Hunt	Harvey B. Hurd	1896
1625 Ashland Ave	Joseph Silsbee	Harvey B. Hurd	1890-91
1631 Ashland Ave	Walter Griffin	Hurd Comstock	1911-12
200 Burnham Place	Handy & Cady	William Hudson Harper	1893
222 Burnham Place	Baumann & Cady	Alice Bunker Stockham	1890-91
2317 Central Park Ave.	Mayo & Mayo	John H. Platt	1927
2411 Central Park Ave.	Granger, Lowe, & Bollenbacher	Olin A. Wakeman	1926
2518 Central Park Ave.	Edgar Ovet Blake	Edgar Ovet Blake	1923
616 Central St.	Ernest Mayo	Betsy A. Bridge	1909
624 Central St.	George W. Maher	Betsy A. Bridge	1909
720 Central St.	Edgar Ovet Blake	Harry E. Brookby	1924
1313 Chancellor St.	Frank Cauley	Richard J. Penny	1940
1317 Chancellor St.	Frank Cauley	Richard J. Penny	1961
1810-12 Chicago Ave.	Stephen Jennings	Robert M. Hatfield	1890
310 Church St.	George W. Maher	A.D. Sheridan	1910
404 Church St.	Mayo & Mayo	Charles P. Whitney	1919
1330 Church St.	Myron Hunt	John Taylor Pirie, Jr.	1898
1414 Church St.	Myron Hunt	George R. Jenkins	1897
1416 Church St.	Walter Griffin	Hurd Comstock	1911-12
625 Clinton Place	Edgar Ovet Blake	Katherine E. Vernon	1923
727 Clinton Place	Childs & Smith	Thomas B. Carson	1912
731 Clinton Place	Childs & Smith	Thomas B. Carson	1912
802 Clinton Place	Childs & Smith	Herbert H. Smith	1915
806 Clinton Place	Fugard & Knapp	John Reed Fugard	1920
810 Clinton Place	Fugard & Knapp	Jay Twitchell	1921
618 Colfax St.	Edgar Ovet Blake	Mary H. Bovee	1915
624 Colfax St.	Edgar Ovet Blake	Arthur C. Burch	1915
628 Colfax St.	Saxe & Zimmerman	David Beaton	1916
629 Colfax St.	Edgar Ovet Blake	George O. Curme	1907
810 Colfax St.	Charles Ayars	Thomas B. Carson	1908

818 Colfax St.	Charles Ayars	Thomas B. Carson	1908
1021 Colfax St.	Edgar Ovet Blake	Leroy H. Sargent	1925
1101 Colfax St.	Frank Cauley	Edward W. Lyons	1926
1911 Colfax St.	William Pocklington	J.B. Finch	1895
2207 Colfax St.	Minard L. Beers	Fred P. Kappelman	1900-1901
2501 Colfax St.	Lowe & Bollenbacher	Elmo C. Lowe	1916
2525 Colfax St.	Granger, Lowe, & Bollenbacher	WilliamJ. Maver	1926
2703 Colfax St.	Robert S. Degoyler	Lowry Grulee	1921
2915 Colfax St.	Frank Cauley	Mary L. Anderson	1925
3005 Colfax St.	Edgar Ovet Blake	Jonh C. McGuire	1931
1220 Crain St.	Charles Ayars	John Schwender	1908
1233 Crain St.	Ernest Mayo	Francis A. Hardy	1909
617 Dartmouth Place	Harry Wheelock	Adam W. Dunn	1909
627 Dartmouth Place	Harry Wheelock	John Brunner	
630 Dartmouth Place	Granger, Lowe, & Bollenbacher	Hugh W. MuCulloch	1925
648 Dartmouth Place	Edgar Ovet Blake	John T. Gascoigne	1913
1301 Davis St.	Perkins & Will	Methodist Church Board of Pensions	1964
1311 Davis St.	Perkins & Will	Methodist Church Board of Pensions	1964
1401 Davis St.	Myron Hunt	Harlow N. Higinbotham	1898-99
1411-15 Davis St.	Myron Hunt	Harlow N. Higinbotham	1898-99
1420 Davis St.	Charles Ayars	Jeannie Lord Ayars	1899
1425 Davis St.	Charles Ayars	William S. Young	1896
115 Dempster	Ernest Mayo	Chester Cook	1911
133 Dempster	Ernest Mayo	Ira Barton Cook	1911
147 Dempster	Chatten & Hammond	George Haskell	1914
221 Dempster	Baumann & Cady	Charles P. Wheeler	1890
413-15 Dempster	Stephen Jennings	Mrs. J.C. Dyke	1896
1327 Dempster	Charles Ayars	Comstock Estate	1906
900 Edgemere Ct.	Mayo & Mayo	Harry N. Selling	1928
917 Edgemere Ct.	Arthur Knox	Antonin Sterba	1922
1415 Elinor Place	Perkins & Hamilton	Eda Hurd Lord	1910
1416 Elinor Place	Perkins & Hamilton	Eda Hurd Lord	1910
1421 Elinor Place	Perkins & Hamilton	Eda Hurd Lord	1909
916 Elmwood Ave.	Charles Ayars	Joel A. Holmgren	1911
917 Elmwood Ave.	Charles Ayars	Joel A. Holmgren	1909
920 Elmwood Ave.	Charles Ayars	Joel A. Holmgren	1911
921 Elmwood Ave.	Charles Ayars	Joel A. Holmgren	1909
925 Elmwood Ave.	Charles Ayars	Joel A. Holmgren	1909
929 Elmwood Ave.	Charles Ayars	Joel A. Holmgren	1909

1139 Elmwood Ave.	Edgar Ovet Blake	Morris C. Plochman	1908
1321 Elmwood Ave.	William Pocklington	Swan Anderson	1893
1401-07 Elmwood Ave.	Stephen Jennings	Thomas Craven	1890
2703 Euclid Park Place	Robert S. Degoyler	Andrew K. Rodgers	1919
2746 Euclid Park Place	Mayo & Mayo	Budd C. Corbus	1922
2756 Euclid Park Place	Chatten & Hammond	James S. Winn	1918
2400 Ewing Ave.	Edgar Ovet Blake	B.C. Burnham	1926
1000 Forest Ave.	Tallmadge & Watson	Frederick S. Kretsinger	1908
1025 Forest Ave.	Ernest Mayo	Edwin Hurlbut	1910
1030 Forest Ave.	Hallberg & Sturm	Charles M. Putnam	1901
1048 Forest Ave.	John T. Wilson Jennings	William Dixon Marsh	1894
1100 Forest Ave.	Beers, Clay & Dutton	Milton H. Wilson	1896
1101 Forest Ave.	Beers, Clay & Dutton	Milton H. Wilson	1896
1120 Forest Ave.	Ernest Mayo	Ernest Reckitt	1909
1140 Forest Ave.	Myron Hunt	James A. Lawrence	1899
1143 Forest Ave.	Stephen Jennings	James W. Donnell	1893
1210 Forest Ave.	Ernest Mayo	Rollins Keyes	1910
1214 Forest Ave.	Ernest Mayo	M.B. Austin	1909
1217 Forest Ave.	Ernest Mayo	George W. Clark	1907
1225 Forest Ave.	Ernest Mayo	Charles H. Barry	1899
1228 Forest Ave.	Franklin Burnham	William H. Burnet	1897
1243 Forest Ave.	H. Ring Clauson	Gordon Copeland	1937
1314 Forest Ave.	Handy & Cady	Albert R. Barhes	1899
1315 Forest Ave.	Tallmadge & Watson	Charles C. Linthicum	1907-1908
1318 Forest Ave.	Ernest Mayo	Frank S. Cunningham	1911
1432 Forest Ave.	Edbrooke & Burnham	David S. Cook	1883
1501 Forest Ave.	Handy & Cady	Frank M. Elliot	1887
1616 Forest Place	George Harvey	Charles G. Ward	1902
629 Garrett Place	Edgar Ovet Blake	Ellen K. French	1916
1114 Grant St.	William Pocklington	Mrs. John J. Foster	1894
3030 Grant St.	Granger, Lowe, & Bollenbacher	James E. Miller	1927
101 Greenleaf St.	Ernest Mayo	Henry Dawes	1913
124 Greenleaf St.	Chester Walcott	Clifford Off	1919
423 Greenleaf St.	Josiah Lane	Charles K. Ober	1895
427 Greenleaf St.	Josiah Lane	Charles K. Ober	1895
144 Greenwood St.	Ernest Mayo	Robert L. Scott	1915
202 Greenwood St.	Joseph Silsbee	Arthur Orr	1889
235 Greenwood St.	Joseph Silsbee	William Hammond	1892
415 Greenwood St.	William Pocklington	Charles H. Harbert	1889

416 Greenwood St.	Stephen Jennings	Henry A. Freeman	1894
516-18 Greenwood St.	William Pocklington	Edward W. Learned	1889
1022 Greenwood St.	Edbrooke & Burnham	George B. Dunham	1883
1028 Greenwood St.	Edbrooke & Burnham	Edwin Hinchliffe	1883
1104 Greenwood St.	Raeder, Coffin, & Crocker	William O. Dean	1892
1311 Grove St.	Perkins & Will	Methodist Church Board of Pensions	1964
208 Hamilton St.	Chatten & Hammond	Edward M. Skinner	1913
225 Hamilton St.	Pond & Pond	Elliot Anthony	1894
2415 Harrison St.	Charles Ayars	A.V. Coffman	1908
2501 Harrison St.	Charles Ayars	Theo W. Chaffee	1910
2523 Harrison St.	Ernest Mayo	Martha Mercer	1899
2715 Harrison St.	Charles Ayars	Otto L. Brownhold	1906
2721 Harrison St.	Arthur Knox	Samuel H. Gilbert	1925
2910 Harrison St.	Lowe & Bollenbacher	Gilbert L. Campbell	1923
2940 Harrison St.	Perkins, Wheeler, & Will	Lawrence B. Perkins	1940
2949 Harrison St.	Perkins, Wheeler, & Will	Philip Will, Jr.	1937
2425 Hartzell St.	Arthur Knox	J. William Link	1927
2512 Hartzell St.	Myron Hunt	Charles Nichols	1899
2522 Hartzell St.	Arthur Knox	Walter Hardy	1912
2714 Hartzell St.	Arthur Knox	Samuel Gilbert	1916
2721 Hartzell St.	Arthur Knox	Carl A. Bessey	1923
2736 Hartzell St.	Edgar Ovet Blake	Daniel W. Allen	1911
625 Haven St.	Lowe & Bollenbacher	F.K. Jackson	1914
1015 Hinman Ave.	Stephen Jennings	Stephen F. ReQua	1894
1022 Hinman Ave.	Ernest Mayo	Mrs. E.E. Nafis	1905
1028 Hinman Ave.	Harry Wheelock	H.W. Rogers	1899
1032 Hinman Ave.	Harry Wheelock	H.W. Rogers	1899
1050 Hinman Ave.	George W. Maher	Mark C. Rasmussen	1917
1109-11 Hinman Ave.	Stephen Jennings	Edward S. Taylor	1892
1115 Hinman Ave.	Harry Wheelock	Mrs. Percy Palmer	1904
1119-21 Hinman Ave.	Edgar Ovet Blake	Hugh A. Ross	1903
1140 Hinman Ave.	Charles Ayars	Arthur M. Shellito	1898
1203-1205 Hinman Ave.	Josiah Lane	Orvis French	1892
1314 Hinman Ave.	Asa Lyon	Eunice Clarinda Reed	1882
1426 Hinman Ave.	Stephen Jennings	Mrs. J.H. Bayliss	1890
1707 Hinman Ave.	William Otis	Humphreys H.C. Miller	1894
1741 Hinman Ave.	John T. Wilson Jennings	G.W. Fowle	1894
583 Ingleside Place	Russell S. Walcott	Johnston A. Bowman	1928
586 Ingleside Park	Tallmadge & Watson	Daniel H. Boone	1925
621 Ingleside Place	Laurence G. Hallberg, Jr.	Samuel Crane Vail	1926
810 Ingleside Place	Edgar Ovet Blake	Ernst V. Anderson	1916

819 Judson Ave.	Edgar Ovet Blake	Willis H. Towne	1910
1024 Judson Ave.	Walter Griffin	Elsie Carter	1910
1041 Judson Ave.	Myron Hunt	John W. Sweet	1897
1045 Judson Ave.	Myron Hunt	John W. Sweet	1897
1114 Judson Ave.	Stephen Jennings	Chester P. Walcott	1892
1122 Judson Ave.	Ernest Mayo	John M. Thomas	1894
1124 Judson Ave.	George Harvey	Charles L. Drain	1896
1135 Judson Ave.	Tallmadge & Watson	Carl S. Jefferson	1912
1142 Judson Ave.	John T. Wilson Jennings	Frank A. Warner	1896
1200 Judson Ave.	Stephen Jennings	S. Frank Wilson	1889
1211-13 Judson Ave.	Josiah Lane	Mary E. Scranton	1892
1215 Judson Ave.	Charles Ayars	Thaddeus W. Heermans	1898
1216 Judson Ave.	William Pocklington	Thaddeus W. Heermans	1890
1217 Judson Ave.	Charles Ayars	Thaddeus W. Heermans	1898
1220 Judson Ave.	Charles Ayars	Frank R. Bissell	1899
1221 Judson Ave.	Charles Ayars	Thaddeus W. Heermans	1898
1225 Judson Ave.	Holabird & Roche	Edwin A. Dawson	1890
1232 Judson Ave.	Stephen Jennings	Frank A. Warner	1889
1235-37 Judson Ave.	Stephen Jennings	William Blanchard	1893
1236 Judson Ave.	Stephen Jennings	Frank A. Warner	1894
1304 Judson Ave.	Josiah Lane	Mrs. J.C. Dyke	1893
1411 Judson Ave.	William Pocklington	Edward S. Turner	1889
1422 Judson Ave.	Holabird & Roche	Frank K. Stevens	1890
1424 Judson Ave.	William Otis	Thomas C. Clark	1902
1512 Judson Ave.	William Pocklington	Mary Scott	1896
1629 Judson Ave.	Handy & Cady	Thomas Creighton	1894
1637 Judson Ave.	Ernest Mayo	Charles P. Whitney	1908
215 Lake St.	Asa Lyon	Michael Tiernan	1881
1000 Lake Shore Blvd.	Tallmadge & Watson	Mrs. Edmund Adcock	1911
1020 Lake Shore Blvd.	Chester Walcott	William R. Johnston	1920
1114 Lake Shore Blvd.	Tallmadge & Watson	Robert Marshall Rolosm	1909
1136 Lake Shore Blvd.	Tallmadge & Watson	Wallace Condict	1909
617 Library Place	Robert C. Spencer, Jr. & Robert R. Kendall	Northwestern University	1894
625 Library Place	Granger, Lowe, & Bollenbacher	Arthur Guy Terry	1925
2200 Lincoln St.	Tallmadge & Watson	Harold G. Peterson	1910
2212 Lincoln St.	Perkins Fellows & Hamilton	Robert A. Worstall	1912
2222 Lincoln St.	Tallmadge & Watson	Charles M. Howe	1909
2319 Lincoln St.	Dwight H. Perkins	Dwight Heald Perkins	1904
2333 Lincoln St.	Perkins & Hamilton	Edwin F. Walker	1908
2404 Lincoln St.	Edgar Ovet Blake	Luther L. Miller	1916
2405 Lincoln St.	Perkins & Hamilton	William A. Colledge	1906

2419 Lincoln St.	Charles Ayars	Charles R. Ayars	1904
2510 Lincoln St.	Clark & Walcott	James Roy Ozanne	1922
2516 Lincoln St.	Lowe & Bollenbacher	Frederick H. Pattee	1923
2525 Lincoln St.	Charles Ayars	Robert E. James	1910
2609 Lincoln St.	Lowe & Bollenbacher	Sidney J. Williams	1919
2610 Lincoln St.	Perkins Fellows & Hamilton	Joseph H. Kearney	1911
2700 Lincoln St.	Perkins Fellows & Hamilton	Charles M. Fairchild	1911
2706 Lincoln St.	Pond & Pond	Charles D. Marsh	1913
2733 Lincoln St.	Edgar Ovet Blake	Howell N. Tyson, Jr.	1925
2221 Lincolnwood Dr.	Arthur Knox	Amelia Jacobson	1925
2447 Lincolnwood Dr.	Granger, Lowe, & Bollenbacher	Justus P. Bauer	1926
732 Madison St.	Stephen Jennings	Nicholas Treff	1893
925 Maple Ave.	Charles Ayars	Axcl F. Carlson	1909-10
930 Maple Ave.	William Pocklington	Adam Thompson	1896
1000 Maple Ave.	Clark & Walcott	John B. Ortlund, Jr.	1922
1011 Maple Ave.	Edgar Ovet Blake	Peter Randler	1903
1023 Maple Ave.	John T. Wilson Jennings	A.L. Currey	1894
1110 Maple Ave.	Ernest Mayo	Nellie Dugdale	1899
1209-17 Maple Ave.	Holabird & Roche	William Blanchard	1892
1214 Maple Ave.	Edbrooke & Burnham	Joseph M. Larimer	1885
1231 Maple Ave.	Stephen Jennings	Jerome A. Smith	1889
1243 Maple Ave.	Charles Ayars	Arthur W. Cooper	1899
2111 Maple Ave.	William Pocklington	Frank Hughes	1895
2127 Maple Ave.	William Pocklington	Charles Beck	1894
2501 Marcy Ave.	H. Ring Clauson	H. Ring Clauson	1937
2514 Marcy Ave.	Tallmadge & Watson	Charlotte M. Heermans	1927
2500 McDaniel Ave.	H. Ring Clauson	Lawrence Kempf	1939
2501 McDaniel Ave.	Perkins, Wheeler, & Will	Sidney J. Williams	1938
633 Michigan Ave. (moved from 919 Judson Ave. in 1946)	Tallmadge & Watson	Chester O. Andrews	1906
926 Michigan Ave.	Tallmadge & Watson	Edward H. Kimbark	1906
930 Michigan Ave.	Myron Hunt	John E. Nolan	1898
1005 Michigan Ave.	Howard Van Doren Shaw	Cyrus Mark	1913
1019 Michigan Ave.	George W. Maher	Thomas B. Carson	1904
1022 Michigan Ave.	George W. Maher	Thomas B. Carson	1909
1023 Michigan Ave.	George W. Maher	Thomas B. Carson	1904
1026 Michigan Ave.	John S. Van Bergen	George S. Ballard	1915
1032-34 Michigan Ave.	Myron Hunt	Nina Drain	1899

1041 Michigan Ave.	John A. Nyden	John Somerville	1916
1042 Michigan Ave.	Josiah Lane	Mrs. Erasmus O. Hills	1895
1046 Michigan Ave.	Josiah Lane	William E. Hills	1895
1110 Michigan Ave.	Holabird & Roche	Robert S. Clark	1890
1126 Michigan Ave.	George Lyons Harvey	William F. Hypes	1897
1133 Michigan Ave.	Perkins, Fellows & Hamilton	John E. Blunt, Jr.	1916
1217 Michigan Ave.	Josiah Lane	William L. Wells	1894
1225 Michigan Ave.	John T. Wilson Jennings	Eugene E. Osborne	1894
625 Milburn St.	Tallmadge & Watson	W.R. Peck	1908
631 Milburn St.	Charles Ayars	Betsy A. Bridge	1909
635 Milburn St.	George W. Maher	Betsy A. Bridge	1909
714 Milburn St.	Ernest Mayo	Williard E. Hotchkiss	1909
719 Milburn St.	Lawrence G. Hallberg, Jr.	Thomas F. Leahy	1923
726 Monroe St.	William Pocklington	Nicholas Kirchsten	1897
806 Monroe St.	William Pocklington	John P. Risch	1897
815-817 Monroe St.	Myron Hunt	Michael L. O'Malia	1901
629 Noyes St.	Childs & Smith	Joseph Pearson	1912
1100 Oak Ave.	W. Carbys Zimmerman	Anna Rew Gross	1901
1106 Oak Ave.	W. Carbys Zimmerman	Anna Rew Gross	1901
1118 Oak Ave.	Tallmadge & Watson	James Wigginton	1908
1228 Oak Ave.	Myron Hunt	William G. Sherer	1898
1560 Oak Ave.	Stephen Jennings	John W. Low	1893
1922 Orrington Ave.	Charles Ayars	Ague C. Griffin	1896
1936 Orrington Ave.	William Pocklington	Ellen E. Langlois	1894
2026 Orrington Ave.	Edgar Ovet Blake	Solon C. Bronson	1903
2030 Orrington Ave.	Edgar Ovet Blake	John A. Scott	1903
2036 Orrington Ave.	Edgar Ovet Blake	Walter Dill Scott	1905
2040 Orrington Ave.	Edgar Ovet Blake	John A. Scott	1905
2103 Orrington Ave.	Josiah Lane	Mary Stevens	1895
2106 Orrington Ave.	William Pocklington	Arthur L. Currey	1895
2110 Orrington Ave.	Edgar Ovet Blake	John A. Scott	1898
2121 Orrington Ave.	Edgar Ovet Blake	Addison B. Phipps	1909
2127 Orrington Ave.	Charles Ayars	James Alden James	1903
2203 Orrington Ave.	William Otis	Northwestern University	1895
2206 Orrington Ave.	Lowe & Bollenbacher	Mrs. M.J. Eastman	1912
2218 Orrington Ave.	Lowe & Bollenbacher	Harold J. Clark	1919
2222 Orrington Ave.	Edgar Ovet Blake	James T. Fulker	1921
2233 Orrington Ave.	Howard van Doren Shaw	Carl E. Williams	1909
2236 Orrington Ave.	Raeder, Coffin, & Crocker	Frank W. McCulloch	1895
2244 Orrington Ave.	Edgar Ovet Blake	Charles W. Spofford	1906
2246 Orrington Ave.	Tallmadge & Watson	Robert K. Row	1915
2320 Orrington Ave.	Edgar Ovet Blake	Ulysses S. Grant	1905

2340 Orrington Ave.	Edgar Ovet Blake	Frederick C. Eiselin	1905
2430 Orrington Ave.	Tallmadge & Watson	Samuel J. Sackett	1927
2436 Orrington Ave.	Ernest Mayo	Sherman C. Kingsley	1909
2505 Orrington Ave.	George W. Maher	Betsy A. Bridge	1909
2525 Orrington Ave.	Edgar Ovet Blake	Christian J. Golee	1924
2608 Orrington Ave.	Edgar Ovet Blake	Ole Johnson	1900
2400 Park Place	Arthur Knox	Arthur Howell Know	1911
2608 Park Place	Edgar Ovet Blake	Royal J. Whitlock	1910
2425 Pioneer Rd.	Spencer & Powers	William G. Leisenring	1915
2444 Pioneer Rd.	Robert C. Spencer, Jr.	Charles A. Whightman	1895
2450 Pioneer Rd.	Robert C. Spencer, Jr.	Charles A. Whightman	1895
2454 Pioneer Rd.	Robert C. Spencer, Jr.	Charles A. Whightman	1895
1041 Ridge Ave.	Tallmadge & Watson	Knowlton L. Ames	1911
1045 Ridge Ave.	Tallmadge & Watson	Knowlton L. Ames	1911
1100 Ridge Ave.	Flanders & Zimmerman	Anna Rew Gross	1897
1110 Ridge Ave.	Zimmerman, Saxe & Zimmerman	Anna Rew Gross	1925
1123 Ridge Ave.	Handy & Cady	William H. Warren	1901
1128 Ridge Ave.	W. Carbys Zimmerman	Henry C. Rew	1898
1139 Ridge Ave.	William C. Pocklington	Gideon Kellogg	1889
1217 Ridge Ave.	Myron Hunt	Chancellor Livingston Jenks, Jr.	1898
1225 Ridge Ave.	Harry Wheelock	Charles G. Neely	1897
1232 Ridge Ave.	Stephen Jennings	William Hugh Jones	1894
1307-13 Ridge Ave.	Myron Hunt	Catherine White	1897
1314 Ridge Ave.	George W. Maher	George B. Dryden	1916
1425 Ridge Ave. (moved from 910 Greenwood St.)	Pond & Pond	Volney W. Foster	1900
1456 Ridge Ave.	Edbrooke & Burnham	John B. Kirk	1884-85
1726 Ridge Ave.	Franklin Burnham	E.C. Ray	1898
2740 Ridge Ave.	Walter Griffin	William Sinclair Lord	1908
2744 Ridge Ave.	Fugard & Knapp	Alf I. Bushnell	1925
2747 Ridge Ave.	Robert S. Degoyler	J.D. W. Archer	1921
2751 Ridge Ave.	Robert S. Degoyler	Cary D. Terrell	1921
2756 Ridge Ave.	Thomas E. Tallmadge	Harry A. Paskind	1938
2757 Ridge Ave.	Robert S. Degoyler	Walter M. Bond	1921
1101 Ridge Rd.	Chatten & Hammond	Horace White Armstrong	1911
815 Ridge Terrace	Childs & Smith	Childs Estate	1915
823 Ridge Terrace	Childs & Smith	Childs Estate	1915
829 Ridge Terrace	Childs & Smith	Childs Estate	1915
2829 Sheridan Place	W. Carbys Zimmerman	Edward K. Warren	1911
2855 Sheridan Place	John A. Nyden	Oscar Haugan	1911

2856 Sheridan Place	Howard Van Doren Shaw	William E. Hall	1927
2864 Sheridan Place	Chester Walcott	Charles J. Traymer	1919
2865 Sheridan Place	Edgar Ovet Blake	Harry E. Byram	1912
2870 Sheridan Place	Tallmadge & Watson	Fred W. Sargent	1926
2878 Sheridan Place	Holabird & Roche	W. Gifford Jones	1915
715 Sheridan Rd.	Lowe & Bollenbacher	Lillian E. Raymond	1910
722 Sheridan Rd.	H. Ring Clauson	John W. Champion	1940
732 Sheridan Rd.	Arthur Knox	Frank Milhening	1920
741 Sheridan Rd.	John S. Van Bergen	Harold R. White	1915
747 Sheridan Rd.	Howard Van Doren Shaw	Harry A. Swigert	1915
936 Sheridan Rd.	Charles Ayars	Jonathan T. Currier	1898
715 Sheridan Rd.	Lowe & Bollenbacher	Lillian E. Raymond	1910
1000 Sheridan Rd.	Mayo & Mayo	John F. Trow	1919
1001 Sheridan Rd.	Lawrence G. Hallberg, Jr.	Sarah L. Vail	1915
1005 Sheridan Rd.	Lawrence G. Hallberg, Jr.	Lawrence G. Hallberg, Jr.	1916
1010 Sheridan Rd.	Chatten & Hammond	John Builder	1911
1027 Sheridan Rd.	George Harvey	Frances M. Erwin	1898
1030 Sheridan Rd.	Ernest Mayo	Thomas Hair	1911
1031 Sheridan Rd.	John T. Wilson Jennings	Charles S. Hannan	1895
1038 Sheridan Rd.	Degolyer & Stockton	T.C. Keller	1925
1046 Sheridan Rd.	Ernest Mayo	Albert H. Williams	1914
1103 Sheridan Rd.	Brown & Wolcott	Edwin Sherman	1912
1110 Sheridan Rd.	Ernest Mayo	Robery E. Wilsey	1912
1117 Sheridan Rd.	Ernest Mayo	Frank Parker Davis	1912
1118 Sheridan Rd.	Ernest Mayo	Achilles H. Reece	1904
1138 Sheridan Rd.	J.K. Cady	Herbery A. Thomas	1890
1139 Sheridan Rd.	W. Carbys Zimmerman	Charles B. Hill	1908
1145 Sheridan Rd.	Tallmadge & Watson	Carroll Shaffer	1913
1201 Sheridan Rd.	Spencer & Powers	Nathan Wilbur Williams	1912
1218 Sheridan Rd.	Ernest Mayo	Frederick E. French	1901
1225 Sheridan Rd.	Ernest Mayo	Wallace Condict	1902
1918 Sheridan Rd.	Robert S. Degoyler	William G. Alexander	1922
1940 Sheridan Rd.	William C. Pocklington	F.W. Beers	1894
2000 Sheridan Rd.	Lowe & Bollenbacher	Frank O. Beck	1921
2016 Sheridan Rd.	William A. Otis	Charles J. Little	1893
2040 Sheridan Rd.	Charles Ayars	Daniel Bonbright	1905
2044 Sheridan Rd.	Dwight H. Perkins	J. Scott Clark	1901
2681 Sheridan Rd.	Stephen Jennings	H.K. Snider	1893
2726 Sheridan Rd.	Ernest Mayo	Charles W. James	1912
2735 Sheridan Rd.	Ernest Mayo	Augusta V. Crawford	1909
2750 Sheridan Rd.	Mayo & Mayo	Charles E. Mallers	1929
2767 Sheridan Rd.	Robert S. Degoyler	Hugh W. McLean	1919
2769 Sheridan Rd.	Robert S. Degoyler	Lorne A. Griffin	1920
1311 Wesley Ave.	Charles Ayars	Comstock Estate	1906
1601 Wesley Ave.	Holabird & Roche	Louis A. Ferguson	1915
1606 Wesley Ave.	Myron Hunt	Harlow N. Higinbotham	1898-99

1621 Wesley Ave.	Myron Hunt	Arthur S. Van Duesen	1897
1627 Wesley Ave.	Myron Hunt	Myron Hunt	1896
1710 Wesley Ave.	Stephen Jennings	Sarah S. Linsley	1894
1721 Wesley Ave.	Josiah Lane	Charles A Wightman	1896
1731 Wesley Ave.	Myron Hunt	Charles A Wightman	1895
1735 Wesley Ave.	Josiah Lane	Charles A. Wightman	1894
1743 Wesley Ave.	Robert C. Spencer, Jr.	Charles A Wightman	1895
1745 Wesley Ave.	Josiah Lane	Charles A Wightman	1897
1814 Wesley Ave.	William C. Pocklington	Alexander Balfour	1895

Selected Bibliography

Anderson, Robert L. *Cooperville Cathedral: The Story of Northminster*. Evanston: Northminster Presbyterian Church, 1973.

Andreas, Alfred Theodore. *History of Chicago, From the Earliest period to the Present Time*. 3 vols. Chicago: A. T. Andreas, 1884-86.

_____. *History of Cook County Illinois*. Chicago: A. T. Andreas, 1884.

Block, Jean F. *Hyde Park Houses: An Informal History, 1856-1910*. Chicago and London: The University of Chicago Press, 1978.

Brooks, H. Allen. *The Prairie School: Frank Lloyd Wright and His Midwest Contemporaries*. Toronto and Buffalo: University of Toronto Press, 1972.

Buckley, James J. *The Evanston Railway Co.* Bulletin 28, Chicago: Electric Railway Historical Society, 1958.

The Bungalow Book, 4th ed. Los Angeles: Henry L. Wilson, 1908.

Cary, Otis. *A History of Christianity in Japan: Protestant Missions*. New York, Chicago, Toronto, London, and Edinburgh: Fleming H. Revell Company, 1909.

Chamberlin, Everett. *Chicago and Its Suburbs*. Chicago: T. A. Hungerford & Company, 1874.

"Chicago in 1856." *Chicago History*, IV, no. 9 (Fall 1956), pp. 257-85.

Clifton, James A. "Chicago, September 13, 1833: The Last Great Indian Treaty in the Old Northwest." *Chicago History*, IX, no. 2 (Summer 1980), pp. 86-97.

Cohen, Stuart E. *Chicago Architects*. Chicago: The Swallow Press Inc., 1976.

Downing, Andrew Jackson. *The Architecture of Country Houses; including Designs for Cottages, Farmhouses, and Villas*. New York: D. Appleton & Co., 1866.

Earhart, Mary. Frances Willard: *From Prayers to Politics*. Chicago: The University of Chicago Press, 1944.

Foster, Clyde D. *Evanston's Yesterdays*. Evanston: n. p., 1956.

French, Frederick E. *Old Evanston and Fifty Years After*. Evanston: Evanston News-Index, 1929.

George, Charles B. *Forty Years on the Rail*. Chicago: R. R. Donnelly & Sons, 1887.

Gordon, Anna Adams. *The Life of Frances E. Willard*. Evanston: National Woman's Christian Temperance Union, 1912.

Grey, Josephine Clarke. *The Grey Family: A History*. Evanston: Privately Printed, 1970.

Hines, Thomas S. *Burnham of Chicago: Architect and Planner*. New York: Oxford University Press, 1974.

Hodgson, Frederick T. *Practical Bungalows for Town and Country*. Chicago: Frederick J. Drake & Company, 1906.

Holt, Glen E. And Dominic A. Pacyga. Chicago: *A Historical Guide to the Neighborhoods. The Loop and South Side*. Chicago: Chicago Historical Society, 1979.

Jacobson, Jacob Zavel. *Scott of Northwestern: The Life Story of a Pioneer in Psychology and Education*. Chicago: L. Mariano, [1951].

Lynes, Russell. *The Tastemakers*. New York: Harper & Brothers, 1954.

Mayer, Harold M. "The Launching of Chicago: The Situation and the Site." *Chicago History*, IX, no. 2 (Summer 1980), pp. 68-79.

_____ and Richard C. Wade. *Chicago: Growth of a Metropolis*. Chicago and London: The University of Chicago Press, 1969.

Monroe, Harriet. *John Wellborn Root: A Study of His Life and Work*. 1896; facsimile edition, Park Forest, Illinois: The Prairie School Press, 1966.

Muggenberg, James "John Van Bergen: The Prairie Spirit into the Mid 20th Century." *Prairie School Review*, XIII (1976), pp. 5-24.

Naruse, Jinzo. *A Modern Paul in Japan: An Account of the Life and Work of the Rev. Paul Sawayama*. Boston and Chicago: Congregational Sunday-School and Publishing Society, [1893].

Our Congregational Heritage. Evanston: First Congregational Church, 1976.

Perkins, Eleanor Ellis. Eve *Among the Puritans: A Biography of Lucy Fitch Perkins*. Boston: Houghton Mifflin Company, 1956.

A Pictorial History of Northwestern University, 1851-1951. Evanston: Northwestern University Press, 1951.

Reeling, Viola Crouch. *Evanston: Its Land and Its People*. Evanston: Fort Dearborn Chapter, Daughters of the American Revolution, 1928.

Schneirov, Richard. "Chicago's Great Upheaval of 1877." *Chicago History*, IX, no. 1 (Spring 1980), pp. 3-17.

Scott, Walter Dill. *John Evans, 1814-1897: An Appreciation*. Evanston: Privately Printed by Courtesy of L. J. Norris, 1939.

Scully, Vincent Joseph, Jr. *The Shingle Style and the Stick Style*. Rev. ed. New Haven and London: Yale University Press, 1971.

Sheppard, Robert D. and Harvey B. Hurd, eds. *History of Northwestern University and Evanston.* Chicago: Munsell Publishing Company, 1906.

Sullivan, Louis Henry. *The Autobiography of an Idea.* New York: W. W. Norton & Company, Inc., 1926.

Tallmadge, Thomas Eddy. "Architectural History of a Western Town." *American Architect and Building News*, CXV, no. 2257 (March 26, 1919), pp. 443-51.

_____. *Architecture in Old Chicago.* Chicago: The University of Chicago Press, 1941.

_____. *The Story of Architecture in America.* New York: W. W. Norton & Company, Inc., 1927.

Wells, Frederic P. *History of Newbury, Vermont.* St. Johnsbury, Vermont: The Caledonian Company, 1902.

Willard, Frances E. *A Classic Town: The Story of Evanston by "An Old Timer."* Chicago: Woman's Temperance Publishing Association, 1891.

Williamson, Harold Francis and Payson Sibley Wild. *Northwestern University: A History, 1850-1975.* Evanston: Northwestern University Press, 1976.

The Woman's Club of Evanston, 75 Sparkling Years: 1889-1964. Evanston: Woman's Club of Evanston, 1964.

In addition, a number of periodicals served as major sources of Evanston history. Among the newspapers the following were the most helpful: *Evanston Index, Evanston Press, Evanston Daily News, Evanston News-Index, Evanston Review, The Nickel's Worth, Chicago Tribune,* and *Chicago Post.* Information from the City of Evanston Building Permits was supplemented by articles and photographs in *Inland Architect, American Architect and Building News, House Beautiful, Architectural Record, Architectural Forum, Brickbuilder,* and *Ladies' Home Journal.*

Index

Illinois Society of Architects, 153
Illinois State Medical Society, 69
Illinois Woman's Centennial Association, 47
Ingraham, Samuel Gilbert "Bert", 118
Ireland, Joseph, 124

Jenks, Chancellor Livingston, 45
Jenks, Chancellor Livingston, Jr., 97, 135, 163
Jenks, O. S., 46
Jenney, William LeBaron, 75, 80, 134, 143
Jenney & Mundie, 148
Jennings, John T. Wilson, 52, 56, 108, 136, 158-162, 164
Jennings, Stephen Alston, 136
Jensen, Jens, 95, 144
Jernegan, Charles, 75
Jernegan, Elizabeth, 76
John Evans Apartments, 107
John M. Smyth & Company, 107, 108
Johnson, Lathrop, 2
Jones, William Hugh, 51, 74, 137, 163
Jones, William Patterson, 17
Judson, Eliza Huddleson, 47
Judson, Philo, 13, 14, 16, 18, 19, 67

Keck, George Fred, 114
Kedzie, John Hume, 71, 72, 78
Kendall, Robert R., 150, 160
Kendall College, 133
Kent, Edward A., 149
Kent College of Law, 126
Keyes, Stephen P., 16
Kidder, Daniel Parish, 16, 18, 62
Kidder, Kathryn, 62
Kidder, Harriet Smith, 16
Kimbark, George, 12
King's College Chapel, Cambridge, England, 112
Kingsley, E. B., 11
Kingsley, Homer Hitchcock, 52, 54
Kingsley, Nellie Fitch, 54, 91
Kirk, James S., 47
Kirkman, Marshall Monroe, 60
Kitchell, Silas, 40
Knapp, George Arnold, 131
Knox, Arthur Howell, 137, 138
Knox College, 11
Kresge Foundation, 111

Yerkes, Charles, 69
Y.M.C.A, 86, 99

1   The photographs taken by Barbara J. Buchbinder-Green are not included in this new edition. New photographs of the properties were taken in 2012 by Jenny Thompson.

2   Viola Crouch Reeling, *Evanston: Its Land and Its People* (Evanston: Fort Dearborn Chapter, Daughters of the American Revolution, 1928), pp. 130-32.

3   Robert D. Sheppard and Harvey B. Hurd, eds., *History of Northwestern University and Evanston* (Chicago: Munsell Publishing Company, 1906), pp. 33-37; Reeling, pp. 132-35.

4   Reeling, pp. 64-65.

5   Alfred Theodore Andreas, *History of Chicago. From the Earliest Period to the Present Time*, 3 vols. (Chicago: A. T. Andreas, 1884-86), I, 51; Sheppard and Hurd, p. 26.

6   Reeling, p. 117.

7   Sheppard and Hurd, pp. 26-27; Reeling, pp. 118-21.

8   James A. Clifton, "Chicago, September 14, 1833: The Last Great Indian Treaty in the Old Northwest," *Chicago History*, IX, no. 2 (Summer 1980), pp. 91-93.

9   Harold M. Mayer, "The Launching of Chicago: The Situation and the Site," *Chicago History,* IX, no. 2 (Summer 1980), pp. 68-78.

10 *Evanston Index* (March 3, 1873); Reeling, pp. 138-41.

11 Reeling, pp. 124-28.

12 Reeling, p. 143.

13 Reeling, p. 169. The final c's were dropped from the name in 1846. "Grosse Point" is the present usage.

14 Reeling, pp. 129-30 and 149-83. The Buckeye Hotel was moved to 1204 Noyes Street in 1916. The roofline has been changed and the structure sheathed in brick so that today it looks like any other bungalow.

15 *Evanston News-Index* (November 26, 1915); Reeling, pp. 167-68. The house was moved to 1016 Colfax Street in 1922, where it still stands, although there have been several additions and remodelings over the years.

16 *Evanston News-Index* (April 15, 1918).

17 Reeling, pp. 164-65.

18 Reeling, pp. 162-64.

19 Reeling, pp. 180-83.

20 The house is illustrated in Reeling, p. 162.

21 Thomas Eddy Tallmadge, *Architecture in Old Chicago* (Chicago: The University of Chicago Press, 1941), pp. 32-34.

22 Tallmadge, pp. 39-40.

23 Tallmadge, pp. 41.

24 Tallmadge, p. 35.

25 Tallmadge, pp. 37-39.

26 Tallmadge, pp. 36.

27 Quoted in Tallmadge, p. 37. Root's article, "The City House in the West," was originally published in *Scribner's Magazine*, VIII, no. 4 (October 1890), pp. 416-34.

28 Andreas, I, 384 and 464-65; Frances E. Willard, *A Classic Town: The Story of Evanston by "An Old Timer"* (Chicago: Woman's Temperance Publishing Association, 1891), pp. 216-17; and Walter Dill Scott, *John Evans, 1814-1897: An Appreciation* (Evanston: Privately Printed by Courtesy of L. J. Norris, 1939), pp. 9-14.

29 "Chicago in 1856," *Chicago History*, IV, no. 9 (Fall 1956), p. 267.

30 Sheppard and Hurd, pp. 463-74.

31 Andreas, I, 518-19. Good moral character was a requisite for membership.

32 Sheppard and Hurd, p. 54; Andreas, I, 223.

33 Sheppard and Hurd, p. 53.

34 Sheppard and Hurd, pp. 53-57; Andreas, I, 219.

35 Sheppard and Hurd, pp. 57-59.

36 Willard, pp. 284-86.

37 See Andreas, I, 187, 216, and 462. Dr. Foster, a veteran of the Black Hawk War, arrived in Chicago in 1830. A member of the Board of Education, in 1857 he gave a thousand dollars to buy "gold, silver or bronze medals or diplomas for the most deserving scholars."

38 Willard, pp. 25-26; Sheppard and Hurd, p. 58; Reeling, pp. 192-93; and Harold Francis Williamson and Payson Sibley Wild, *Northwestern University: A History, 1850-1975* (Evanston: Northwestern University Press, 1976) pp. 8-9.

39 See "Chicago in 1856," p. 276.

40 Jean F. Block, *Hyde Park Houses: An Informal History, 1856-1910* (Chicago and London: The University of Chicago Press, 1978), p.3.

41 Reeling, pp. 196-97; Willard, p. 219. However, according to John Evans' obituary in the *Evanston Index* (July 10, 1897), "it is said that the daughter of Orrington Lunt was asked to arbitrate the question, and she named the town Evanston." The Plat of Evanston was recorded on July 27, 1854.

42 Sheppard and Hurd, p. 62; Reeling, pp.197 and 201. See also *Evanson Press*, (January 26, 1889) and August 31, 1889.

43 Tallmadge, p. 63. According to the *Evanston Review* (February 22, 1951), it was Van Osdel & Bowman.

44 Frederic P. Wells, *History of Newbury, Vermont* (St. Johnsbury, Vermont: The Caledonian Company, 1902), pp. 212-13; Sheppard and Hurd, pp. 61-62. In 1871 the Preparatory, or Old College as it came to be called, was moved to the campus and enlarged. In 1899 it was moved further north when Fisk Hall was built. Old College survived until 1973 when Northwestern demolished it.

45 Willard, p. 30. In 1847 it was merged into the General Biblical Institute at Concord, New Hampshire; it ultimately became the School of Theology at Boston University. See also Wells, pp. 217-18.

46 Willard, pp. 31-32; Reeling, pp. 229-33. Dempster Hall burned down in 1879.

47 Willard, pp. 83-87; Reeling, p. 235.

48 Sheppard and Hurd, p. 68.

49 Mary Earhart, *Frances Willard: From Prayers to Politics* (Chicago: The University of Chicago Press, 1944), pp. 98 and 391, note 15.

50 Willard, pp. 60-62; Reeling pp. 208-209.

51 Willard, pp. 22-23 and pp. 231-36; Reeling, p. 241.

52 Reeling, pp. 201-202.

53 Sheppard and Hurd, pp. 246-47.

54 Willard, p. 394; Clyde D. Foster, *Evanston's Yesterdays* (Evanston: n. p., 1956), pp. 14-16. See also the 1860 Federal Census, dwelling no. 224; and *Evanston Press* (May 17, 1902). In 1868 Maria Murray married George Robinson and they set up housekeeping at 325 Dempster Street. Upon her death in 1900, she was buried in Rosehill Cemetery next to Mrs. Vane; see *Evanston Index* (May 19, 1900).

55 Willard, p. 231; Sheppard and Hurd, p. 334.

56 Willard, pp. 373-74.

57 Willard, pp. 223-24; Sheppard and Hurd, p. 247.

58 Sheppard and Hurd, pp. 247-48.

59 Willard, pp. 378-79; Sheppard and Hurd, pp. 250-51.

60 Sheppard and Hurd, p. 474; *Evanston Press* (February 21, 1891).

61 Willard, pp. 329-30; Sheppard and Hurd, p. 248.

62 Willard, p. 69.

63 *Evanston Review* (March 15, 1951).

64 Reeling, pp. 389-90; Willard, p. 20.

65 Reeling, pp. 390-92.

66 Sheppard and Hurd, p. 170.

67 Sheppard and Hurd, pp. 170-71.

68 Sheppard and Hurd, pp. 176-77.

69 Sheppard and Hurd, p. 20; Reeling, p. 199.

70 Willard, pp. 19-20.

71 Sheppard and Hurd, p. 342.

72 Reeling, pp. 264-67.

73 Reeling, pp. 271-82.

74 Sheppard and Hurd, pp. 375-76.

75 Sheppard and Hurd, pp. 65 and 317.

76 Willard, p. 167.

77 Willard, p. 167.

78 Sheppard and Hurd, p. 65.

79 Williamson and Wild, p. 6.

80 Robert D. Sheppard and Harvey B. Hurd, eds., *History of Northwestern University and Evanston* (Chicago: Munsell Publishing Company, 1906), p. 16.

81 Quoted in Harold Francis Williamson and Payson Sibley Wild, *Northwestern University: A History, 1850-1975* (Evanston: Northwestern University Press, 1976) p. 35.

82 Viola Crouch Reeling, *Evanston: Its Land and Its People* (Evanston: Fort Dearborn Chapter, Daughters of the American Revolution, 1928), p. 408.

83 Walter Dill Scott, *John Evans, 1814-1897: An Appreciation* (Evanston: Privately Printed by courtesy of L. J. Norris, 1939), p. 49.

84 Reeling, p. 257.

85 Reeling, p. 234; Harold M. Mayer and Richard C. Wade, *Chicago: Growth of a Metropolis* (Chicago and London: The University of Chicago Press, 1969), p. 95.

86 Frances E. Willard, *A Classic Town: The Story of Evanston by "An Old Timer"* (Chicago: Woman's Temperance Publishing Association, 1891), pp. 176-84; Reeling, pp. 408-26.

87 Willard, p. 183; Reeling, p. 423. Jane Currie Hoge wrote *Heroes of the Rank and File and Boys in Blue* about her experiences.

88 From Harriet Kidder's journal, quoted in Willard, pp. 181-82; see also Reeling, p. 422. Both authors call her only Mrs. Hyde (Hide), but the 1860 census provided her name. The first part of the Emancipation Proclamation was issued on September 22, 1862. The entirety of the proclamation went into effect on January 1, 1863.

89 *Evanston Index* (August 7, 1897.)

90 Willard, p. 69, Reeling, p. 344. According to state statute, a town could be no larger than one mile square.

91 Reeling, p. 344.

92 *Evanston Index* (February 13, 1909).

93 *Evanston Press* (May 11, 1889). In 1873 the Northwestern Female College building was converted to a hotel—Lakeside Hall.

94 Willard, p. 63.

95 Reeling, pp. 219-20.

96 Anna Adams Gordon, *The Life of Frances E. Willard* (Evanston: National Woman's Christian Temperance Union, 1912), p. 56.

97 Mary Earhart, *Frances Willard: From Prayers to Politics* (Chicago: The University of Chicago Press, 1944), pp. 98-102.

98 Willard, pp. 62-64; Reeling, p. 220; and Earhart, p. 103.

99 Willard, p. 65; Earhart, pp. 110-11; Williamson and Wild, p. 29; and Reeling, pp. 220-22.

100 Earhart, pp. 113 and 392-93.

101 Williamson and Wild, p. 40, quoting *Chicago Republican* (September 9, 1869).

102 Willard, p. 49.

103 Willard, pp. 312-14.

104 Willard, p. 298; Sheppard and Hurd, pp. 329 and 604-606; *Evanston Press* (February 16, 1889).

105 *Evanston Index* (June 22, 1872) and (September 7, 1895); Sheppard and Hurd, pp. 484-85.

106 Willard, pp. 154-55.

107 Willard, pp. 155-57; Sheppard and Hurd, p. 434.

108 Willard, pp. 240-50.

109 Willard, pp. 368-71.

110 *Evanston Index* (January 19, 1895); see also Otis Cary, *A History of Christianity in Japan: Protestant Missions* (New York, Chicago, Toronto, London, and Edinburgh: Fleming H. Revell Company, 1909), pp. 13 and 132. Rev. Greene was honored by the Emperor of Japan and became a member of the Japanese court; see *Evanston Daily News* (May 19, 1913).

111 See Jinzo Naruse, *A Modern Paul in Japan: An Account of the Life and Work of the Rev. Paul Sawayama* (Boston and Chicago: Congregational Sunday-School and Publishing Society, [1893]).

112 Sheppard and Hurd, p. 165.

113 Reeling, p. 259.

114 Willard, p. 166.

115 Willard, p. 167.

116 Sheppard and Hurd, p. 318.

117 Willard, pp. 168-69 and 224-27.

118 Willard, p. 169; Earhart, pp. 138-43.

119 Charles F. Grey, in conversation with J. Seymour Currey, January 26, 1900 (Evanston History Center files).

120 Willard, pp. 169 and 224-27.

121 The house was remodeled in 1928 by Mayo & Mayo and no longer bears any resemblance to the original structure.

122 Earhart, pp. 64-65.

123 In 1994, the WCTU formed the Frances Willard Historical Association, which oversees the "Rest Cottage" (now known as the Frances Willard House Museum), library and archives. On October 15, 1966, the house was designated a National Historic Landmark.

124 Vincent Joseph Scully, Jr., *The Shingle Style and the Stick Style*, rev. ed. (New Haven and London: Yale University Press, 1971), p. xxviii.

125 Andrew Jackson Downing. The Architecture of Country Houses; including Designs for Cottages, Farm-Houses, and Villas (New York: D. Appleton & Co., 1866), p. v-vi.

126 Downing, p. 27.

127 Downing, p. 28.

128 Scully, p. xxix.

129 Scully, pp. xxxi-xxxii.

130 Quoted in Scully, p. xxxiii.

131 Downing, pp. 257-58.

132 Thomas Eddy Tallmadge, "Architectural History of a Western Town," *American Architect and*

Building News, CXV, no. 2257 (March 26, 1919), p. 446.

[133] The White house is still standing, but has undergone many alterations by its successive owners. It is known today as Lohr Park; the main house was converted to condominiums and several small houses were built on its once spacious grounds.

[134] Sheppard and Hurd, p. 80

[135] Sheppard and Hurd, pp. 84-85.

[136] Frederick E. French, *Old Evanston and Fifty Years After* (Evanston: Evanston News-Index, 1929), p. 11.

[137] French, pp. 12-15. It was demolished in 1952.

[138] According to Edith P. Welch who lived in the house from 1928 to 1964.

[139] Sheppard and Hurd, pp. 297-98.

[140] Henry C. Tillinghast bought the property for his father-in-law in 1872 and retained ownership until 1883. See also Silas H. Kitchell's obituary, *Evanston Index* (December 1, 1877).

[141] Sheppard and Hurd, p. 553. The house was demolished February 1949.

[142] Willard, p. 372.

[143] Reeling, pp. 396-99. Sewell was also the publisher of *The Little Corporal*, a popular children's magazine. Among those who worked with him on the magazine were Edward Eggleston, who established Evanston's first kindergarten in a little building adjacent to his home at the corner of Davis Street and Oak Avenue, and John and Emily Huntington Miller. She was the first woman trustee to serve on Northwestern's executive committee.

[144] Sheppard and Hurd, pp. 289-90; *Evanston Index* (March 14, 1874).

[145] Sheppard and Hurd, pp. 337-38.

[146] *Evanston Index* (May 5, 1877).

[147] Sheppard and Hurd, p. 183; Reeling, p. 394.

[148] *Evanston Index* (October 19, 1872). The keeper's house was finished by May 1873 and the lighthouse was operating in March 1874. On September 8, 1976, the lighthouse complex was entered on the National Register of Historic Places.

[149] Sheppard and Hurd, pp. 151-52.

[150] Sheppard and Hurd, p. 17; Willard; p. 69; Reeling, p. 345.

[151] *Evanston Index* (July 27, 1872), (January 11, 1873), (February 1, 1873), and (September 19, 1874); Sheppard and Hurd, pp. 17-18.

[152] *Evanston Index* (September 27, 1873).

[153] French, p. 42.

[154] The pumping engine's brass nameplate is part of the collection of the Evanston History Center.

[155] Mrs. Samuel Peeney recalled that when she and her husband moved to North Evanston in 1867 there were only nine houses; see *Evanston Index* (December 31, 1918).

[156] *Evanston Index* (August 10, 1872).

[157] Reeling, p. 345; see also *Evanston Index* (August 10, 1872).

[158] *Evanston Index* (March 28, 1874).

[159] *Evanston Index* (July 21, 1873).

[160] *Evanston Index* (March 11, 1874); see also Sheppard and Hurd, pp. 251-52.

[161] *Evanston Index* (February 21, 1874) and (April 25, 1874).

[162] *Evanston Press* (September 25, 1891); see also Charles B. George, *Forty Years on the Rail* (Chicago: R. R. Donnelley & Sons, 1887), p. 93.

[163] *Evanston Press* (September 28, 1891); Alfred Theodore Andreas, *History of Cook County Illinois* (Chicago: A. T. Andreas, 1884), p. 456.

[164] Everett Chamberlin, *Chicago and Its Suburbs* (Chicago: T. A. Hungerford & Company, 1874), p. 376.

[165] Letter to J. Seymour Currey, dated December 1, 1902 (Evanston History Center files.)

166   Sheppard and Hurd, p. 175; Andreas, p. 456.

167   Willard, pp. 422-23; Reeling, p. 313.

168   Sheppard and Hurd, p. 176; Reeling, p. 247.

169   Reeling, pp. 347-48; see also *Evanston Review* (July 4, 1963).

170   *Evanston Index* (February 7, 1874).

171   *Evanston Index* (April 25, 1874). In the Village of Evanston 447 people voted for the annexation.

172   Richard Schneirov, "Chicago's Great Upheaval of 1877," *Chicago History*, IX, no. 1 (Spring 1980), pp. 3-4.

173   Schneirov, p.17.

174   Schneirov, pp. 3-17.

175   *Evanston Index* (August 13, 1887).

176   Robert D. Sheppard and Harvey B. Hurd, eds., *History of Northwestern University and Evanston* (Chicago: Munsell Publishing Company, 1906), p. 191. See also *Evanston Index* (September 18, 1875) and (September 25, 1875); the high school opened in September 1875, but the number of students soon crowded the elementary classes and space was found in the second floor rooms over the post office. The high school department later moved next door to Lyons Hall.

177   *Evanston Index* (January 28, 1882), (February 18, 1882), and (February 25, 1882).

178   Frances E. Willard, *A Classic Town: The Story of Evanston by "An Old Timer"* (Chicago: Woman's Temperance Publishing Application Association, 1891), p. 144; Sheppard and Hurd, pp. 193-95; Reeling, p. 324. Boltwood had organized the first township high school in the state at Princeton in 1867 and later another at Ottawa.

179   *Evanston Press* (June 20, 1891); *Evanston Index* (June 20, 1891).

180   Sheppard and Hurd, p. 549; Viola Crouch Reeling, *Evanston: Its Land and Its People* (Evanston: Fort Dearborn Chapter, Daughters of the American Revolution, 1928), pp. 312-13.

181   Sheppard and Hurd, p. 192; *Evanston Press* (March 24, 1894) and (September 5, 1896).

182   City of Evanston Building Permit #419, March 29, 1894; it was demolished in 1936.

183   Sheppard and Hurd, p. 191. After the death of school board president Humphreys H. C. Miller in 1910, it was renamed in his honor.

184   *American Architect and Building News*, LIII (July 25, 1896), plate 1074.

185   *Evanston Index* (June 2, 1894). The new building was designed by Thomas & Rapp. It was demolished in 1960.

186   Sheppard and Hurd, p. 192; *Evanston Index* (September 15, 1894). It was built by William C. Pocklington.

187   Reeling, p. 446.

188   Sheppard and Hurd, p. 192.

189   Sheppard and Hurd, p. 397.

190   Willard, p. 173; Sheppard and Hurd, pp. 399-400.

191   Willard, p. 173.

192   See Harold M. Mayer and Richard C. Wade, *Chicago: Growth of a Metropolis* (Chicago and London: The University of Chicago Press, 1969), p. 160.

193   Sheppard and Hurd, pp. 604-606; *Evanston Press* (March 28, 1896). The Marcy Home was built at the corner of Maxwell and Newberry streets in Chicago.

194   Harold Francis Williamson and Payson Sibley Wild, *Northwestern University: A History, 1850-1975* (Evanston: Northwestern University Press, 1976), pp. 86 and 125. Wilson donated $25,000 in 1901.

195   Glen E. Holt and Dominic A. Pacyga, *Chicago: A Historical Guide to the Neighborhoods. The Loop and South Side* (Chicago: Chicago Historical Society, 1979), p. 126.

196   *Evanston Index* (January 16, 1897); *Evanston News-Index* (January 15, 1916).

197   *Evanston Index* (October 2, 1880); Sheppard and Hurd, pp. 631-62.

198   Sheppard and Hurd, pp. 405-407. The house, completely remodeled in 1902 for M. Cochrane Armour by Harry Bergen Wheelock, was demolished in 1930.

199   Willard, p. 58.

200   Sheppard and Hurd, pp. 580-81.

201   Sheppard and Hurd, pp. 258.

202   *Evanston Press* (January 5, 1889).

203   Reeling, p. 345.

204   Sheppard and Hurd, pp. 415-17.

205   Sheppard and Hurd, pp. 260-65.

206   *Evanston Index* (February 16, 1878).

207   *Evanston Index* (September 2, 1882).

208   Willard, p. 414; see also *Evanston Index* (March 5, 1887) and (March 19, 1887).

209   Sheppard and Hurd, p. 436.

210   Sheppard and Hurd, pp. 437-38.

211   Sheppard and Hurd, pp. 453-61.

212   Sheppard and Hurd, pp. 449-52. The clubhouse was demolished in 1958.

213   Sheppard and Hurd, pp. 443-47 and 559-62; see also Willard, pp. 367-68; *The Woman's Club of Evanston, 75 Sparkling Years: 1889-1964* (Evanston: Woman's Club of Evanston, 1964), pp. 1-4; *Evanston News-Index* (January 20, 1925.)

214   Sheppard and Hurd, pp. 276 and 279-81.

215   Sheppard and Hurd, p. 281-82; *Evanston Index* (August 25, 1905).

216   *Evanston Press* (May 24, 1890). After his appointment to the faculty of the University of Chicago, Taft moved to Hyde Park.

217   *Evanston Press* (September 19, 1891). See also Kathryn Kidder's scrapbook in the Evanston History Center files.

218   Some credit Garwood with the "sundae," while Newton P. Williams is another druggist who may have been the so-called inventor. Garwood moved into the store on the corner of Fountain Square in the fall of 1881 and left the city in 1903. Up until the time of his death in Seattle, Washington, in 1939, he made no mention of the "sundae." See *Evanston News-Index* (January 18, 1939) and (November 26, 1939). The source of the legend is explained in Clyde D. Foster, *Evanston's Yesterdays* (Evanston: n. p., 1956), pp. 89-91; it was perpetuated in the *Evanston Review* (July 4, 1963).

219   *Evanston Index* (September 2, 1882).

220   Williamson and Wild, p. 51; *Evanston Index* (February 19, 1887).

221   Williamson and Wild, pp. 51-53; *Inland Architect*, XI (May 1888).

222   Williamson and Wild, p. 78.

223   Williamson and Wild, p. 71.

224   Sheppard and Hurd, p. 94.

225   Reeling, p. 226; Williamson and Wild, p. 85; and especially the chapter written by Peter Christian Lutkin in Sheppard and Hurd, pp. 131-48.

226   Sheppard and Hurd, p. 143.

227   Sheppard and Hurd, p. 139-40 and 576-77.

228   William and Wild, p. 86.

229   Sheppard and Hurd, pp. 149-50.

230   Sheppard and Hurd, p. 235; see also *Brickbuilder*, IV (August 1895), pp. 1798-80.

231   Williamson and Wild, pp. 96 and 82; *Evanston Press* (May 16, 1896).

232   *The Nickel's Worth* (June 26, 1888). This was the second and final issue of South Evanston's only

newspaper.

233 Sheppard and Hurd, pp. 495-97.

234 *Evanston Press* (January 2, 1892).

235 *Evanston Press* (April 30, 1892).

236 *Evanston Press* (February 27, 1892) and *Evanston Index* (February 29, 1892).

237 *Evanston Press* (April 23, 1892).

238 *Evanston Press* (April 23, 1892).

239 Mayer and Wade, p. 177.

240 *Evanston Press* (April 21, 1894).

241 Sheppard and Hurd, pp. 503-505; see also *Evanston Index* (August 20, 1904); *Evanston Press* (August 20, 1904); and Foster, pp. 160-62.

242 *Evanston Index* (November 30, 1895). It was predicted that "the motorcycle is the machine of the road for the future." See also *Evanston News-Index* (January 24, 1920) and (January 28, 1921); *Evanston Review* (January 4, 1963). However, Reeling, p. 387, says Edwin F. Brown owned the first automobile in Evanston.

243 James J. Buckley, *The Evanston Railway Co.*, Bulletin 28 (Chicago: Electric Railway Historical Society, 1958), p. 8.

244 Buckley, p. 13; *Evanston Press* (May 2, 1896).

245 Buckley, p. 37.

246 *Evanston Index* (April 10, 1880): "Evanston is popularly known to the outside world as Saints' Rest. Railway men sometimes jocularly direct the godly to Hevanston, and shunt the ungodly off to Helgin."

247 *Evanston Index* (January 7, 1882), (January 14, 1882), and (February 4, 1882).

248 Vincent Joseph Scully, Jr., *The Shingle Style and the Stick Style*, rev. ed. (New Haven and London: Yale University Press, 1971), pp. lii-lix.

249 *Evanston Index* (September 23, 1882) and (November 4, 1882).

250 *Evanston Index* (July 1, 1882).

251 *Evanston Index* (December 3, 1881). It was demolished in 1967 and the site turned into St. Mark's Court.

252 *Evanston Index* (February 11, 1882).

253 *Inland Architect*, I (April 1883), p. 35. The house was totally remodeled for Rufus F. Dawes in 1916 by Ernest A. Mayo. It is now Northwestern's John Evans Alumni Center.

254 *Evanston Index* (August 18, 1883).

255 *Evanston Press* (November 29, 1890).

256 *Evanston Index* (Christmas Number, 1886).

257 *Evanston Index* (October 22, 1892); *Inland Architect*, XX (November 1892).

258 *Evanston Index* (January 26, 1895); *Inland Architect*, XXVI (January 1896); City of Evanston Building Permit #451, June 18, 1894.

259 *Evanston Press* (May 9, 1891).

260 Alfred Theodore Andreas, *History of Cook County Illinois* (Chicago: A. T. Andreas, 1884), pp. 451-52; *Evanston Press* (May 24, 1890), said of one of Pocklington's designs, "The style of the house is peculiar, being different from most of Evanston houses."

261 Scully, p. 88.

262 Thomas Eddy Tallmadge, "Architectural History of a Western Town," *American Architect and Building News*, CXV, no. 2257 (March 26, 1919), p. 447; see also *Inland Architect*, XIV (December 1889).

263 *Evanston Press* (November 29, 1890).

264 *Inland Architect*, XXXIV (September 1899).

265 City of Evanston Building Permit #940, January 11, 1896, *Evanston Index* (September 29, 1900). Burnham was the company architect of Joseph Sears' Kenilworth Company and designed a number of houses and the Chicago North Western Railroad station in that suburb.

266 See *Evanston Index* (September 1, 1906). Dawes House was designated a National Historic Landmark on December 8, 1976.

267 The house was demolished in 1969.

268 *Evanston Index* (May 28, 1887); Thomas S. Hines, *Burnham of Chicago: Architect and Planner* (New York: Oxford University Press, 1974), pp. 250-51.

269 Hines, pp. 125-26.

270 Burnham & Root designed houses for Hugh R. Wilson, George S. Lord, Clara Burnham Woodyatt, Thomas Lord, Dr. Charles G. Fuller, P. J. Kasper, and William L. Brown.

271 *Inland Architect*, II (November 1883), p. 133.

272 *Evanston Index* (May 16, 1891); *Evanston Press* (May 23, 1891) and (June 11, 1892). See also Harriet Monroe, *John Wellborn Root: A Study of His Life and Work* (1896; facsimile edition, Park Forest, Illinois: The Prairie School Press, 1966), p. 285; *Inland Architect*, XXIV (October 1894).

273 See Hines, pp. 73-124.

274 Louis H. Sullivan, *The Autobiography of an Idea* (New York: W. W. Norton & Company, Inc. 1926), p. 325.

275 *Evanston Index* (January 26, 1901), (September 14, 1901), and (September 21, 1901).

276 *Evanston Index* (January 19, 1901). In 1900 the death rate was 10.3 per 1,000 residents.

277 *Evanston Index* (January 5, 1901).

278 *Evanston Index* (April 14, 1900) and (December 10, 1910.)

279 *Evanston Index* (November 21, 1914).

280 *Evanston Index* (April 6, 1907). In the election for justice of the peace, she beat her male opponent by a vote of 2,226 to 971.

281 Rev. Hugh Elmer Brown, Funeral Service, First Congregational Church, April 1945; see also *Evanston Review* (April 26, 1945.)

282 *Evanston Daily News* (June 12, 1913), (June 13, 1913), (June 14, 1913), and (June 15, 1913).

283 *Evanston Index* (June 12, 1909) and (September 25, 1909).

284 *Evanston News-Index* (March 17, 1916).

285 *Evanston Daily News* (April 28, 1913); *Evanston News-Index* (July 11, 1914).

286 *Evanston Index* (October 23, 1909), (January 29, 1910), and (October 22, 1910); *Evanston News-Index* (February 14, 1914).

287 *Evanston News-Index* (March 11, 1915).

288 Robert D. Sheppard and Harvey B. Hurd, eds., *History of Northwestern University and Evanston* (Chicago: Munsell Publishing Company, 1906), pp. 201-202.

289 *Evanston Index* (January 17, 1903); *Evanston News-Index* (May 20, 1916).

290 See Eleanor Ellis Perkins, *Eve Among the Puritans: A Biography of Lucy Fitch Perkins* (Boston: Houghton Mifflin Company, 1956), pp. vii-xi and 224-32.

291 *Chicago Sunday Tribune* (October 14, 1934); *Evanston News-Index* (November 1, 1937).

292 *Evanston News-Index* (January 28, 1921).

293 *Evanston Index* (December 12, 1914).

294 Harold Francis Williamson and Payson Sibley Wild, *Northwestern University: A History, 1850-1975* (Evanston: Northwestern University Press, 1976), pp. 110-11.

295 *Evanston Index* (May 19, 1909), (May 29, 1909), (June 5, 1909), and (June 1, 1912).

296 *Evanston News-Index* (June 28, 1919).

297 *Evanston News-Index* (January 15, 1934).

298   *Evanston News-Index* (December 23, 1932).

299   *Evanston Press* (January 23, 1897); Josephine Clarke Grey, *The Grey Family: A History* (Evanston: Privately Printed, 1970), pp. 14-16.

300   *Evanston Review* (July 4, 1963).

301   *Evanston Index* (August 19, 1911).

302   See *Our Congregational Heritage* (Evanston: First Congregational Church, 1976), pp. 188-90; *Evanston Review* (February 12, 1942).

303   Evanston Daily News (May 29, 1913).

304   *Evanston News-Index* (August 8, 1914), (August 15, 1914), and (August 22, 1914). They were released after two hours.

305   See the Evanston History Center files on both men.

306   Williamson and Wild, p. 133.

307   Jacob Zavel Jacobsen, *Scott of Northwestern: The Life Story of a Pioneer in Psychology and Education* (Chicago: L. Mariano, [1951]), pp. 83-123; Williamson and Wild, p. 133.

308   *Evanston News-Index* (January 9, 1919).

309   He was killed on September 17, 1918; see *Evanston News-Index* (October 4, 1918); *Chicago Post* (February 7, 1919); *Evanston News-Index* (May 19, 1924).

310   *Evanston News-Index* (April 28, 1920).

311   Garnett was killed in battle on October 29, 1918; Garnett Place was dedicated Sunday, May 22, 1938. It was once thought that Garnett was the first and only African-American Evanstonian killed in World War I. However, Corporal Wayman Guinn died August 9, 1918, the first of Evanston's African-American soldiers "to die in service"; *see Evanston News-Index* (August 29, 1918).

312   Evanston News-Index (May 1, 1919).

313   H. Allen Brooks, *The Prairie School: Frank Lloyd Wright and His Midwest Contemporaries* (Toronto and Buffalo: University of Toronto Press, 1972), pp. 28-29.

314   Letter from Dwight H. Perkins to Margery B. Perkins, August 21, 1940.

315   Ibid.

316   Louis H. Sullivan, *The Autobiography of an Idea* (New York: W. W. Norton & Company, Inc., 1926), Chapter XII.

317   *Evanston Press* (December 15, 1894).

318   City of Evanston Building Permit #864, June 17, 1896.

319   City of Evanston Building Permit #1057, September 11, 1897; *Inland Architect*, XXXIV (November 1899); *House Beautiful*, XVII (May 1905), p. 27.

320   City of Evanston Building Permit #2461, August 14, 1905. This "Evanston Model Home" developed from a design that Wright did for *Ladies' Home Journal*.

321   *Evanston News-Index* (March 15, 1917); City of Evanston Building Permit #7407, March 20, 1917.

322   City of Evanston Building Permit #2099, March 31, 1904. See also *Architectural Record*, XVIII (1905), pp. 71-72.

323   Brooks, pp. 112-14.

324   Brooks, pp. 71, 118, 166-69, 238, and 262. Griffin also designed a fifth house in Evanston, a summer cottage for William S. Lord at 2740 Ridge Avenue.

325   Brooks, pp. 79-80, 165, and 284-85.

326   James Muggenberg, "John Van Bergen" The Prairie Spirit into the Mid 20th Century," *Prairie School Review*, XIII (1976), pp 7-8; Brooks, p. 85; *Evanston News-Index* (March 2, 1917).

327   Brooks, p. 102; see also *Ladies' Home Journal*, XXVII (August 1910), p. 29.

328   Thomas Eddy Tallmadge, *Architecture in Old Chicago* (Chicago: The University of Chicago Press, 1941), pp. x-xi.

329   Thomas Eddy Tallmadge, *The Story of Architecture in America* (New York: W. W. Norton & Company, Inc., 1927), p. 233.

330   *See House Beautiful*, X (November 1901), pp. 231-38.

331   *Evanston Index* (December 7, 1907) and (August 21, 1909).

332   Brooks, pp. 67 and 109-10; *Evanston Index* (February 22, 1908). Three years later Northwestern chose the campus plan by the New York architectural firm of Palmer & Hornbostel; Maher's plan came in third place; see *Evanston Index* (April 29, 1911).

333   Tallmadge, *America*, p. 233.

334   Tallmadge, *America*, pp. 214-33. In 1922 George Grant Elmslie designed the last Prairie School house in Evanston; it was built at 2700 Grant Street for James Montgomery (City of Evanston Building Permit #9946, June 30, 1922).

335   Quoted in Russell Lynes, *The Tastemakers* (New York: Harper & Brothers, 1954), p. 188.

336   *Evanston Index* (January 9, 1909).

337   *The Bungalow Book*, 4ᵗʰ ed. (Los Angeles: Henry L. Wilson, 1908), pp. 4-5. It first appeared about 1907 and soon ran into five editions.

338   Frederick T. Hodgson, *Practical Bungalows and Cottages for Town and Country* (Chicago: Frederick J. Drake & Company, 1906), pp. 3-4. In this edition he was assisted by architect Ernest Newton Braucher, who designed a number of houses in Evanston.

339   In particular, see 2301, 2303, 2309, 2311, 2313, and 2321 Thayer Street.

340   City of Evanston Building Permit #1685, January 31, 1901.

341   *Evanston Press* (November 30, 1901).

342   *Evanston Press* (December 14, 1901); *Evanston Index* (January 4, 1902).

343   See *Evanston Review* (May 7, 1953).

344   Evanston Daily News (May 8, 1913).

345   *Evanston Daily News* (May 7, 1913); *Evanston Index* (March 21, 1914); *Evanston Daily News* (November 18, 1914).

346   *Evanston News-Index* (January 14, 1915).

347   *Evanston News-Index* (February 16, 1916), (June 7, 1916), and (June 10, 1916).

348   *Evanston News-Index* (May 17, 1916) and (November 13, 1916).

349   *Evanston News-Index* (December 12, 1916).

350   *Evanston News-Index* (January 15, 1916).

351   *Evanston News-Index* (March 11, 1916), (April 28, 1916), and (June 10, 1916).

352   *Evanston News-Index* (August 19, 1916).

353   *Evanston News-Index* (March 11, 1916), (March 25, 1916), and (April 19, 1916).

354   *Evanston News-Index* (November 26, 1918).

355   *Evanston News-Index* (January 19, 1921).

356   *Evanston News-Index* (January 1, 1921), (January 15, 1921), (January 19, 1921), and (April 1, 1921).

357   *Evanston News-Index* (August 15, 1921).

358   *Evanston News-Index* (August 22, 1921).

359   *Evanston News-Index* (January 9, 1922); City of Evanston Building Permit #9458, January 9, 1922.

360   City of Evanston Building Permit #10704, January 19, 1923; *Evanston News-Index* (September 24, 1923).

361   City of Evanston Building Permit #14321, August 15, 1925; *Evanston News-Index* (January 24, 1925.)

362   City of Evanston Building Permit #18005, May 17, 1928.

363   City of Evanston Building Permit #14701, December 23, 1925; *Evanston News-Index* (December 7, 1925) and (January 20, 1927).

364   *Evanston News-Index* (February 24, 1927) and (February 8, 1928).

365 It was demolished in December 1975; see *Evanston Review* (December 11, 1975.)
366 City of Evanston Building Permit #12055, January 14, 1924.
367 City of Evanston Building Permit #10208, July 29, 1922; *Evanston News-Index* (September 25, 1923).
368 *Evanston Review* (March 4, 1926.)
369 *Evanston News-Index* (March 1, 1929), (April 22, 1929), and (November 23, 1929).
370 City of Evanston Building Permit #22883, February 20, 1940; *Evanston Index* (February 21, 1940). The building was designed by Mundie, Jensen, Bourke & Havens. See also *Evanston Review* (February 6, 1941).
371 *Evanston Review* (August 9, 1945), (October 31, 1946), and (March 4, 1948).
372 *Evanston Review* (November 10, 1949) and (November 17, 1949).
373 *Evanston Review* (July 5, 1951).
374 *Evanston Review* (July 1, 1976).
375 "Dedication Program of the Municipal Building. Evanston, Illinois, January 6, 1947."
376 *Evanston Review* (June 4, 1953).
377 *Evanston Review* (November 26, 1936). In 1958, Graham, Anderson, Probst & White redesigned the entrance and completed a seven-story addition to Washington National's building at 1630 Chicago Avenue. The building was demolished in the early 1990s by developer John Buck Co. It was replaced with The Park Evanston and nearby Whole Foods Market, completed in 1997 and designed by Harry Weese Architects.
378 *Evanston Review* (January 29, 1953) and (February 26, 1953).
379 *Evanston Review* (February 12, 1953).
380 *Evanston Review* (March 26, 1953).
381 *Evanston Review* (May 28, 1953).
382 *Evanston Review* (August 6, 1953).
383 *Evanston Review* (November 25, 1954).
384 Evanston Chamber of Commerce, "Evanston Industrial Directory," March 1, 1968.
385 *Evanston Review* (February 10, 1966) and (February 17, 1966).
386 League of Women Voters of Evanston, "This is Evanston," 6th ed. (Evanston, 1976), p. 22.
387 Williamson and Wild, pp. 107-108.
388 Williamson and Wild, p. 146.
389 Williamson and Wild, pp. 151, 161, 182, 201-202, 217, and 220.
390 Williamson and Wild, pp. 199 and 217.
391 Williamson and Wild, p. 220.
392 *A Pictorial History of Northwestern University*, 1851-1951 (Evanston: Northwestern University Press, 1951), p. 179.
393 Williams and Wild, pp. 261 and 272-73.
394 Williamson and Wild, pp. 262-63 and 274-80.
395 Williamson and Wild, pp. 280-81.
396 *Evanston Review* (November 20, 1969).
397 *Evanston Review* (April 11, 1974).
398 *Evanston Review* (October 13, 1977).
399 City of Evanston Building Permit #20268, August 14, 1931. Perkins, who had not yet received his license, was working for his father's firm of Perkins Chatten & Hammond, the name on the permit.
400 City of Evanston Building Permit #21828, June 15, 1937. No architect is named on the permit.
401 Stuart E. Cohen, *Chicago Architects* (Chicago: The Swallow Press Inc., 1976), p. 21-25.
402 *Evanston Review* (September 22, 1936), (September 24, 1936), and (September 28, 1936); City of Evanston Building Permit #21554, September 24, 1936.

403 Robert L. Anderson, *Cooperville Cathedral: The Story of Northminster* (Evanston: Northminster Presbyterian Church, 1973), pp. 110-12; City of Evanston Moving Permit #757, April 19, 1951.

404 City of Evanston Building Permit #21844, July 26, 1937; see also *Architectural Forum*, LXXI (October 1939), pp. 242-43).

405 City of Evanston Building Permit #23628, September 22, 1941.

406 *Evanston Review* (April 6, 1944).

407 *Evanston Review* (June 15, 1944), (November 23, 1944), and (November 30, 1944).

408 *Evanston Review* (July 4, 1946).

409 City of Evanston Building Permit #38517, April 3, 1968. The Chicago Chapter of the American Institute of Architects honored the Haid house with a 1970 Distinguished Building Award.

410 City of Evanston Building Permit #41011, July 10, 1973. The Chicago Chapter of the American Institute of Architects honored the Wilson house with a 1975 Distinguished Building Award. See also *Inland Architect*, n.s., XIX, no. 9 (September 1975), pp. 14-17.

411 City of Evanston Building Permit #41502, April 25, 1974.

412 The Larson house was designed by Jerome R. Gentile Jr.

Made in the USA
Monee, IL
22 August 2022